**Collins**

Student Support
Materials for **AQA**

AS and A-level
# Sociology

# Education
# with Research
# Methods

Authors: Martin Holborn and Nichola McConnell

Collins. Freedom to teach.

An imprint of HarperCollins*Publishers*
The News Building
1 London Bridge Street
London
SE1 9GF

Browse the complete Collins catalogue at
**www.collins.co.uk**

ISBN 978-0-00-822163-8

British Library Cataloguing in Publication Data.

A catalogue record for this publication is available
from the British Library.

Commissioned by Catherine Martin

Developed by Jo Kemp

Edited by: Kate Ellis

Project managed by Sadique Basha at Jouve

Original design by Newgen Imaging

Typeset by Jouve India Private Limited

Cover design by Ink Tank

Cover image by OFFFSTOCK/Shutterstock

Production by Lauren Crisp

Printed and bound by Martins the Printers

Indexed by Jouve

**Acknowledgements**

Every effort has been made to contact the holders of
copyright material, but if any have been inadvertently
overlooked the publishers will be pleased to make the
necessary arrangements at the first opportunity.

p 4, source: Office for National Statistics; p 12, source:
Office for National Statistics; p 20, source: Office for
National Statistics; p 28, source: Office for National
Statistics; p 39, Table 9, source: Office for National
Statistics; p 43, source: Office for National Statistics; p
65, Table 18, source: Home Office.

Thanks to the following students for providing answers
to the first edition questions:

Ruby Barwood, Collette Blackman, Lauren Foley, Vicki
Gill, Jessica Gowers, Fran Guratsky, Rachel Hewitt, Ella
Keating, Charlotte Ross, Eric Wedge-Bull.

Thanks to Peter Langley for his work as series editor on
the first edition.

# Contents

## Introduction to the education system

### The growth of state education

In the UK, free compulsory state education started in 1870, although since 1833 the state had made some contribution to funding education.

- In 1880 state education was made compulsory up to the age of 10.
- By 1918 children had to stay at school until the age of 14, and in 1972 the school leaving age was raised to 16.
- Anyone born after 1 September 1997 has to stay in education or training until they are 18.
- Higher education has also expanded rapidly, so that over 40% of school leavers now go on to study at that level.

A variety of sociological perspectives have examined the role of education in society and discussed the reasons for the expansion of state education.

## The functionalist perspective

Functionalists see society as an interrelated whole. To functionalists every institution in society performs one or more important **functions** or jobs and they assume that this helps society to run smoothly like a well-oiled machine. Functionalist theories of education therefore look for the positive benefits and functions that education performs for all societies.

## Durkheim – education and social solidarity

Émile Durkheim (1925) saw the main role of education as the transmission of the **norms** and **values** of society. Education helps to unite all individuals within society, creating a sense of belonging and commitment to that society, or what Durkheim called **social solidarity**. By the teaching of history, individuals learn about their society and develop a sense of commitment to it.

Durkheim saw schools as societies in miniature in which individuals learn to interact with others and follow a fixed set of rules. This provides preparation for later life when individuals will have to get on with others and adhere to rules in society.

Durkheim also believed that education helps to teach the specific skills necessary in an **industrial society** with specialist jobs (an advanced **division of labour**), which could not be taught by parents, who lack the specialist knowledge.

### Examiners' notes

On AS Paper 1, you can get a whole range of questions on **functionalism**, including 2-, 6-, 10- and 20-mark questions. 2-mark questions might ask you to 'Define a term', which could be any of the concepts in bold on these pages, so knowing the glossary terms is important.

For A-level Paper 1, you could be asked a 4-, 6-, 10- or 30-mark question related to functionalism.

### Examiners' notes

You are unlikely to be asked specifically about one functionalist writer, but when answering longer questions on both AS and A-level papers, it is helpful to make reference to all three of the functionalists discussed in this section to pick up maximum marks for knowledge and understanding.

### Key study
### Parsons: universalistic values

Talcott Parsons (1961) believed education has three main functions.

1. It is a bridge between the family and wider society.
2. It socializes children into the basic values of society.
3. It selects people for their future roles in society.

Before attending school, children are socialized within the family where **particularistic standards** are used; that is, children are treated as particular individuals. In society as a whole, however, **universalistic standards** are usually used, in which people are judged according to standards that apply equally to everybody.

In families, **status** is fixed by birth; this is **ascribed status**. However, in society as a whole, status is based on **merit** (for example, people compete to get jobs) and status is therefore achieved.

Parsons believed that education makes the transition from family to society as a whole possible by getting people used to universalistic values and **achieved status**.

Education socializes individuals into the major values of society, the belief in **individual achievement** and in the value of **equality of opportunity**. The exam system encourages these values because it judges people fairly and motivates them to be successful.

Education also assesses students' abilities so that they can be matched to suitable jobs, allowing them to make a major contribution to society.

## Davis and Moore – education and role allocation

Davis and Moore (1945) viewed education as a means of **role allocation**. Education sifts and sorts people according to their abilities so that the most able gain high qualifications and can progress to doing the most **functionally important jobs** in society. The most important jobs are more highly rewarded, thereby motivating the talented to work hard to achieve those positions. In this way, education helps to ensure that competent people fulfil the important roles in society and are motivated to work hard. Davis and Moore saw education as **meritocratic**; that is, people are judged according to their ability and effort, not according to who they are.

## Criticisms of functionalism

The main criticisms of functionalism are summarized in **Table 1**.

| Functionalist view | Criticism |
|---|---|
| Education benefits society as a whole | **Marxists** argue that education benefits the **ruling class** (see page 6), while **feminists** see it as benefiting men (see page 24) |
| Education promotes the norms and values of society as a whole (Durkheim, Parsons) | Marxists see education as promoting the values of powerful groups. Hargreaves (1982) believes education promotes **competition** and **individualism** rather than shared values |
| Education promotes social solidarity (Durkheim) | Education can be divisive because of a **hierarchy** of schools and universities, which can separate **social classes** |
| Educational achievement is based on merit | A great deal of research shows that class, gender and ethnicity influence achievement |
| Education selects the most appropriate people to do particular jobs (Davis and Moore) | Other factors apart from qualifications influence the **labour market** (e.g. social contacts – who you know) |

Table 1
Criticisms of functionalism

**Examiners' notes**

The functionalist theories can be compared and contrasted with other theories such as Marxism or **feminism**, especially in 20-mark AS questions and 30-mark A-level questions, in order to gain evaluation and analysis marks.

**Essential notes**

There has been an immense amount of research on whether society really is meritocratic, and most of it has concluded that meritocracy is a myth. For example, your social class background seems to influence both the qualifications and the jobs that you get independently of your ability or achievements in education.

## Introduction to Marxism

According to Karl Marx (1818–1883) and Frederick Engels (1820–1895) **power** in society largely stemmed from wealth. In particular, those who owned the **means of production** (the things needed to produce other things such as land, **capital**, machinery and labour power) formed a powerful ruling class. They were able to exploit the **subject class** (those who did not own the means of production and therefore had to work for the ruling class).

## Economic systems

According to Marx, society passed through several eras in which different economic systems or **modes of production** were dominant. In each of these there was a different ruling class and subject class. In the latest stage, **capitalist society**, the ruling class were wealthy factory owners (the **bourgeoisie**) and the subject class were the working-class employees (the proletariat). In **capitalism** the proletariat was exploited by the bourgeoisie because they were not paid the full value of the work that they did and the bourgeoisie kept some **surplus value** or profit.

## The economic base and superstructure

The power of the bourgeoisie derived from their ownership of the means of production. The means of production forms the **economic base** or **infrastructure** of society. Because they controlled the economic base, the bourgeoisie were able to control the other, non-economic, institutions of society (which make up the **superstructure**), such as the media, government, religion, the family and education.

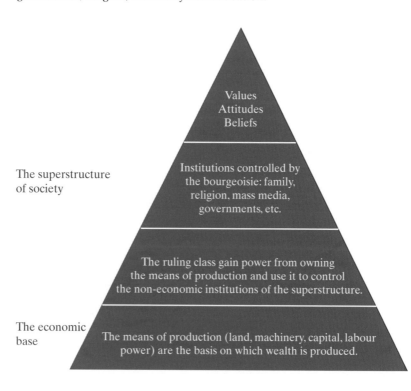

The superstructure of society

Values
Attitudes
Beliefs

Institutions controlled by the bourgeoisie: family, religion, mass media, governments, etc.

The ruling class gain power from owning the means of production and use it to control the non-economic institutions of the superstructure.

The economic base

The means of production (land, machinery, capital, labour power) are the basis on which wealth is produced.

**Fig 1**
A Marxist model of society

## Key study
## Bowles and Gintis: Capitalist schooling

Bowles and Gintis (1976) argue that education is controlled by capitalists and serves their interests. There is a close relationship between schooling and work, because schooling is used to prepare children for working in capitalist businesses. The **correspondence principle** states that education corresponds to employment.

### The hidden curriculum

Capitalism requires a hard-working, obedient workforce that will not challenge the management. Bowles and Gintis believe that education prepares such a workforce through the **hidden curriculum**. This works in the following ways:

- Conformist pupils are awarded higher grades than those who challenge authority or think creatively.
- Schools teach acceptance of hierarchy, since teachers give the orders and pupils obey.
- Pupils are motivated by the **external rewards** of exam success just as workers are motivated by wages.
- Both work and education are **fragmented**, or broken into small pieces, so that workers and pupils have little overall understanding of production or society. This keeps them divided.

Bowles and Gintis see the idea of **meritocracy** as a myth and, in reality, class background as determining how well a person does. However, because people believe that the education system is meritocratic, this **legitimates** the system, making it seem fair.

## Criticisms of Marxism

Marxism in general, and Bowles and Gintis in particular, have been criticized in a number of ways.

| Marxist view | Criticism |
|---|---|
| Education corresponds to work | Brown et al. (1997) believe that much work now requires teamwork rather than obedience |
| Education creates obedient and uncritical workers | Reynolds (1984) believes that some education encourages critical thinking (e.g. sociology) Some neo-Marxists such as Willis believe that the hidden curriculum is not always accepted |
| Education is controlled by capitalists | Elected local education authorities and teachers have some independence and do not have to follow the wishes of capitalists |
| Education only benefits the ruling class | Functionalists believe that education benefits society as a whole, while feminists believe that it benefits men rather than the ruling class |
| Evidence supports the Marxist theory (Bowles and Gintis) | The research by Bowles and Gintis is dated, USA-focused and may not apply to today |

**Examiners' notes**

This is a vital study, which is useful for answering any 10- or 20-mark AS questions and 10- or 30-mark A-level questions about the Marxist view of the role of education in society.

**Examiners' notes**

You could well be given a 20-mark AS or 30-mark A-level question asking you to describe and evaluate the Marxist and Marxist-feminist perspective. In this case, make sure you bring in neo-Marxism and Marxist feminism as well, to get into the top mark band for skills of interpretation, application, analysis and evaluation.

**Essential notes**

Neo-Marxist views are examined in the next section and provide partial support for Bowles and Gintis, but also offer a more sophisticated and developed viewpoint.

**Table 2**
Criticisms of Marxism

**Examiners' notes**

Alternative perspectives, which are developed in much more detail in other sections will allow you to add substance to many of these criticisms. To support Marxism you can point out that there is a good deal of research, which suggests that education is not meritocratic but influenced by social class.

## Neo-Marxism and education

**Neo-Marxism** is a term used to describe new versions of Marxism. They are new (neo) because they disagree in some way with the original writings of Karl Marx, while still being strongly influenced by them.

## Giroux – neo-Marxism, struggle and relative autonomy

An example of neo-Marxism applied to education is the work of Henry Giroux (1984). He disagrees with the conventional Marxist approach of Bowles and Gintis (see previous pages) in three ways.

1. Working-class pupils do not passively accept everything they are taught, but actively shape their own education and sometimes resist the discipline imposed on them by school.
2. Schools are **sites of ideological struggle** for different classes, ethnic, religious and cultural groups. Capitalists have more power than any other single group but they do not have all the power.
3. The education system possesses **relative autonomy** from the economic base; that is, it has some independence and is not always shaped by the needs of the capitalist economy.

### Examiners' notes

Including neo-Marxism will give you a better chance of getting into the top mark band in 20-mark AS and 30-mark A-level questions. It allows you to evaluate other perspectives and include high-level analysis in all theory questions.

### Examiners' notes

Although old, this is an invaluable study. It is useful for answering Research Methods questions on observation or interviews. It is the main example for illustrating neo-Marxism and can be used to develop and to evaluate the Marxist perspective. It can also be used in many answers on processes within schools and to explain why boys may do poorly in education.

### Key study
### Willis: Learning to Labour

The most influential neo-Marxist study of education is an **ethnographic study** of a group of boys (or 'lads') in a Midlands **comprehensive school** in the 1970s. Paul Willis (1977) conducted the study using **interviews**, **observation** and **participant observation** in the school.

- The 'lads' saw themselves as superior to staff and other pupils.
- They were not interested in getting academic qualifications.
- They aimed to do as little work as possible while entertaining themselves through bad behaviour.
- They were unhappy at being treated as children and identified more with the adult world.
- They formed a **counterculture**, which was **sexist** (looking down on women) and **racist** (looking down on ethnic minorities). They valued traditional **working-class masculinity**, which emphasized toughness and despised weakness.
- Physical, **manual labour** was seen as more valuable than 'pen-pushing'.

### Shop-floor culture and the counter-school culture

Willis followed the lads into their first jobs, often in factories. He found a **shop-floor culture** similar to the **counter-school culture**, which

- was racist and sexist
- had little respect for authority.

Workers did as little work as possible and tried to enjoy themselves through, 'having a laff'. They developed ways of coping with boring work over which they had little control. Paul Willis argues that to some extent the lads saw through the capitalist system, perceiving that they had little chance of progressing through hard work in education to well-paid or high status jobs.

However, he also saw that their actions led them into jobs where they were exploited by the ruling class.

**Examiners' notes**

Do not forget to criticize the study for its small unrepresentative sample and for being dated if you use it in longer answers.

## Comparison and evaluation of Marxism and neo-Marxism

**Table 3** compares and evaluates the work of the most influential Marxists, Bowles and Gintis and the most influential neo-Marxist, Paul Willis.

**Examiners' notes**

This table is useful for providing high-level analysis, necessary for the top mark band in longer questions.

| Marxism – Bowles and Gintis | Neo-Marxism – Paul Willis |
|---|---|
| **Key concepts** | |
| The correspondence principle, the hidden curriculum, the myth of meritocracy | Counter-school culture, shop-floor culture, 'having a laff' |
| **Relationship between capitalism and education** | |
| Capitalism directly shapes the content of education and controls the behaviour of pupils | Capitalism shapes society as a whole but groups within education form their own subcultures |
| **View of pupil behaviour** | |
| Pupils conform within school | Some pupils actively rebel against school |
| **Relationship between school and work** | |
| Schools create passive, obedient workers who will be easily exploited | Schools creates poorly behaved workers, but workers who do not rebel against the capitalist system as a whole |
| **Main strengths** | |
| Analyzes the overall relationship between education and capitalist society | Based on detailed ethnographic research. Shows a subtle understanding of behaviour in schools. Does not assume that most pupils conform |
| **Main weaknesses** | |
| Based on limited evidence. Exaggerates the control of capitalists over education. Doesn't examine the positive benefits of education or explore gender inequalities within education | Dated, and based on a very small sample. Oversimplifies school subcultures into two types: pro- and anti-school. Relies too much on Willis' own interpretation of the lads' behaviour |

**Table 3**
Comparison and evaluation of Bowles and Gintis, and Willis

## Introduction

Functionalist, Marxist and neo-Marxist perspectives are all based on specific sociological theories, but some views of the relationship between education and society are based more on political **ideologies** and associated social policies relating to the education system. Two such approaches are the **social democratic** and **neoliberal** perspectives. Social democratic perspectives are more **left wing** (in favour of greater equality and greater state intervention in the economy) and the neoliberals are more **right wing** (in favour of competition and **free markets**).

## Social democratic perspectives on education

From this perspective, governments should play a major role in providing welfare through the **state** for its citizens in order to promote the well-being of members of society. Society produces inequality of **income** and wealth, which creates **inequality of opportunity**. Those from advantaged backgrounds tend to do better in the education system.

The role of the state should be to make opportunity more equal and society more **meritocratic**. In a meritocracy, success and failure in education and in the labour market are based on effort and ability.

Social democratic perspectives influenced Labour governments of the 1960s and 70s. They were opposed to the **tripartite** system in which pupils went to one of three types of school:

- **grammar schools**, which provided an academic education for those who had passed the 11+ exam
- **secondary modern schools**, which provided a more vocational education
- **technical schools**, for those with technical ability.

Grammar schools were **selective**, taking only higher-ability pupils. Social democrats believe this system was divisive because most pupils in grammar schools were from **middle-class** backgrounds, whereas most in secondary modern schools were from working-class backgrounds.

## Social democratic policies

The Labour governments of the 1960s and 70s partly replaced the tripartite educational system with comprehensive schools which all pupils attended. The intention was to

- get rid of class divisions between different types of schools
- create more equal opportunities
- encourage economic growth by ensuring that talent was not wasted through sending talented pupils to secondary modern schools where they would not develop their skills fully.

The Labour government also worked to reduce inequality in society through taxation and welfare policies in which the rich were more heavily taxed than others (**progressive taxation**), and welfare was provided to the less well-off so that they did not live in **poverty**.

## Neoliberal perspectives on education

Neoliberals (also sometimes called the **New Right**) are opposed to the views of social democrats.

The neoliberals believe:
- **Private enterprise**, based on competition between businesses, is the most efficient system for running any service.
- Services provided by the state tend to be inefficient. This is because the producers have no incentive to work hard since, unlike business, there is no competition.
- There are no customers paying for the service, meaning that state education is unresponsive to its customers.
- Competition is essential to raising standards, which is vital if the UK is to produce the highly educated adults who are necessary to compete in the global economy.
- The main focus of education should be on training the workforce.
- Training the workforce requires a new emphasis on **vocational** education.

## Neoliberal policies

The neoliberal perspective on education influenced the policies of the Conservative governments of Margaret Thatcher and John Major from 1979 to 1997. The main features of these policies were:
- They introduced market forces and competition between educational institutions.
- Schools competed for pupils, and unpopular schools lost money.
- Greater **choice** was introduced with new types of schools such as **grant-maintained schools** funded directly by the government.
- The **National Curriculum**, **league tables**, regular inspections and frequent testing were all designed to drive up standards in order to make the UK more economically competitive.

## Social democratic and neoliberal perspectives compared

**Table 4** outlines the main similarities and differences, and strengths and weaknesses of these perspectives.

| Social democratic perspective | Neoliberal perspective |
| --- | --- |
| **Aim of education** | |
| To promote greater equality, reduce class divisions and promote economic growth. To provide equality of opportunity | To raise standards and promote economic growth. To train the workforce needed by business |
| **Policies supported** | |
| Comprehensive schools, growing welfare state, higher income tax for the rich | Competition and parental choice in education, reduced state expenditure |
| **Governments influenced** | |
| Labour governments of 1960s and 70s | Conservative governments of 1979–97 and Coalitions/Conservative governments 2010–15 and post-2015 |
| **Ideology** | |
| Left wing, seeing state and redistribution of wealth as desirable | Right wing, seeing a small state and private enterprise as desirable |

### Essential notes

The neoliberals believe that raising standards will promote economic growth, but this is best achieved through competition rather than spending more government money.

### Examiners' notes

If you are asked about education and the economy, discuss the neoliberal argument that too much spending on education will lead to higher taxes, which will prevent economic growth.

### Examiners' notes

If you are asked a 20-mark AS or 30-mark A-level question about neoliberals you can expand on the material here by using the discussion of policies found on pages 38–39.

### Examiners' notes

Do not forget that in any question asking you to evaluate a theory, including Marxism and functionalism, these perspectives can be brought in to provide contrast and criticism.

Table 4
Social democratic and neoliberal perspectives compared

☞ This topic continues on the next two pages

## Introduction

**Differential educational achievement** refers to differences in the level of educational qualification achieved by social groups.

Social classes can be defined in a number of ways, but all definitions are based on the idea that groups in society can be divided according to their economic circumstances. For example, income, wealth and occupation are frequently seen as the most important factors distinguishing social classes.

On this basis, three main classes can be distinguished:

1. The **upper class**, who own significant amounts of wealth; for example, land, property, businesses or shares.
2. The middle class, who have **non-manual** jobs (that is, their jobs primarily involve mental rather than physical labour) with relatively high pay and job security. They usually have higher-level qualifications.
3. The working class, who have manual jobs (their jobs primarily involve physical labour). They do not usually have higher-level qualifications and on average have lower pay and less job security than the middle class.

## Evidence of class inequality in differential achievement

Class inequalities in differential achievement are usually measured through a comparison of classes based on **occupational groups**.

A wide range of data shows continuing and significant inequalities in educational achievement by social class. The Youth Lifestyles Survey of 2010 found that

- only 7% of 16-year-olds from the highest-class background (higher professional) failed to get level 2 qualifications, compared with 30% from the lowest-class background (routine occupations)
- 77% of children from the highest class achieved level 3 (e.g. A-level) qualifications, but only 38% of children from the lowest class
- 60% of highest-class children went on to higher education (19% at the most prestigious universities), compared with 22% of lowest-class children (a mere 4% at the most prestigious universities).

These differences have not significantly reduced in recent years.

The evidence therefore shows a large and persistent gap between the educational attainment of higher and lower classes.

A variety of theories have been used to explain inequalities in achievements:

- Some have emphasized **cultural factors**, while others have emphasized **material factors** (that is, differences in income and resources).

- Some have emphasized factors in the education system itself, whereas others have emphasized factors outside the education system.

## Class subcultures and educational achievement

A number of theories emphasizing factors outside the education system have blamed the underachievement of the working class in education on the inadequacy of working-class culture, particularly inside working-class homes. These theories are known as **cultural deprivation** theories (the working class are deprived of the **culture** necessary for educational success).

Early research by sociologists such as David Lockwood (1966) claimed to identify distinctive **subcultures** associated with the middle class and the working class.

**Examiners' notes**

It is quite common to get 20- or 30-mark questions asking you to evaluate whether cultural or material factors are more important, or alternatively whether factors inside or outside the education system are most important. Make sure you know which categories each approach comes into.

**Table 5**
Social class subcultures

|  | Working class | Middle class |
|---|---|---|
| **Time orientation:** | Present-time orientation – live life in the moment rather than worrying about the future | **Future-time orientation** – think ahead rather than living in the moment |
| **Attitude to gratification:** | Seek **immediate gratification** – enjoy yourself now (e.g. spending your wage packet as soon as you are paid) | **Deferred gratification** – put off pleasure now in order to achieve greater pleasure in the future (e.g. saving for a deposit on a house) |
| **Collectivism versus individualism:** | Success achieved through collective action (e.g. a union going on strike) | Success achieved through individual action (e.g. studying or working hard) |
| **Attitudes to luck:** | Your chances in life are based on luck or fate (**fatalism**) | Your chances in life are based on ability and hard work: you make your own luck |

**Examiners' notes**

You will not need to go through all these differences in detail, but you should use the main concepts and outline the differences if you need to discuss cultural factors that affect educational achievement.

It is debatable how far these **class subcultures** still exist today, but some sociologists have argued that there are still differences in social class subcultures and these might affect educational achievement.

- Barry Sugarman (1970) argues that the **present-time orientation** and inability to defer gratification of the working class makes them unlikely to sacrifice immediate income in order to stay on in education to gain higher wages and a better job in the longterm.
- In addition, the fatalism of the working class means they generally do not believe that they can improve their prospects through their own hard work.
- The collectivist approach makes them less likely to pursue individual success through the education system.

☞ **This topic continues on the next two pages**

**Examiners' notes**

This is a useful example of a longitudinal study to refer to in answers about research methods applied to education.

## Key study
## Douglas: Cultural deprivation

In an influential **longitudinal study**, J.W.B. Douglas (1964, 1970) followed the careers of over 5000 children through the education system. Douglas found that working-class parents showed less interest in their children's education than middle-class parents. For example, working-class parents

- visited school less often to discuss their children's progress
- were less keen than the middle class for their children to stay on at school after the minimum leaving age.

Douglas also found that working-class parents gave their children less attention and stimulation during their early years. He therefore believed that differences in **primary socialization** between the social classes explained the relative educational failure of the working class.

More recent research by Feinstein (2003) used data from the National Child Development Study to examine the effects of cultural and other factors in shaping educational achievement. Feinstein found:

- Financial deprivation (having poorer parents) had some effect on achievement.
- Cultural deprivation was much more important, and the extent to which parents encouraged and supported their children was the crucial factor in determining how well they did.

In 2010, Goodman and Gregg analyzed research from four longitudinal studies to investigate why poverty was associated with low educational achievement. They found that cultural factors played a key role, for example, the quality of mother–child interactions and how often parents read books to children both influenced achievement. The value that parents put on education was also important, as was the extent to which parents got involved in their children's schooling.

### Evaluation of cultural deprivation theory

Cultural deprivation theory has been heavily criticized. Blackstone and Mortimore (1994), for example, argue that

- research has not measured parental interest in education adequately. Teachers' assessments have often been used and these may not reflect the real level of interest of parents.
- working-class parents may feel less able to visit school because they feel uncomfortable interacting with middle-class teachers.
- schools with more middle-class children tend to have more organized systems of parent–school contacts.

Goodman and Gregg's 2010 research found that cultural factors were not the only thing that influenced attainment – material factors and child–teacher interactions also had an effect.

**Examiners' notes**

Cultural deprivation theory has been heavily criticized because it seems to blame the working class for a system which disadvantages them. Make sure that you point out the weaknesses of the theory in all 20- and 30-mark answers.

## Key study
## Basil Bernstein: Speech patterns

Bernstein (1972) believes that a particular aspect of culture – speech – shapes educational achievement. He distinguishes two types of speech patterns:

- **Restricted codes** – are a type of shorthand speech in which meanings are not made fully explicit. They are characterized by short, simple and often unfinished sentences. This type of speech code is more typical of the working class, who are more likely than the middle class to communicate verbally in their jobs and less likely to need to write reports.
- **Elaborated codes** – are types of speech in which the meanings are filled in and made explicit; sentences tend to be longer and more complex. These are more likely to be used in middle-class jobs where there is a greater requirement to write reports and produce **documents**.

In education, elaborated codes are necessary for exam success in many subjects, and as teachers are themselves middle class they are more likely to use elaborated codes. Being socialized in households that largely use restricted codes holds back the working class in the education system, making it more difficult for them to achieve academic success.

Bernstein, however, has been criticized by Gaine and George (1999). They argue that

- Bernstein oversimplifies the differences between middle- and working-class speech patterns.
- many other factors apart from speech affect educational attainment.
- class differences in speech patterns have declined since Bernstein did his research.

**Examiners' notes**

You may be asked to use an example to explain how cultural deprivation can cause underachievement (AS 2-mark question) or outline three ways in which the working class may be culturally deprived (AS 6-mark question). You may be asked to outline three cultural factors that can cause differential achievement (A-level 6-mark question) or to analyze or outline and explain two processes outside school that can cause differential achievement in class (10-mark question). Speech patterns, parental involvement in education and primary socialization are good examples that you can use for these types of questions.

## Compensatory education

Although cultural deprivation theory has been heavily criticized, it has influenced a range of educational policies. These policies have led to the idea of positive discrimination in the form of **compensatory education** – the working class are given extra help in the education system to compensate for the inadequacy of their socialization. In recent decades, a variety of schemes have provided extra help for the working class. These range from **Education Action Zones** in the 1970s, to **Sure Start**, which since 1998 has provided additional pre-school education to try to compensate for any lack of educational stimulation from parents.

Critics such as Whitty (2002) believe that all these schemes place blame for failure on the child and her or his background and ignore the effects of inequality in society as a whole. Many schemes have lacked resources and have failed to tackle the poverty that is the underlying cause of educational inequality.

**Examiners' notes**

This could feature in a short question. It can also be useful for developing the evaluation of cultural deprivation, since policies based upon the theory have had limited effectiveness.

## Bourdieu: Capital and educational achievement

Some sociologists accept that culture can play a part in educational achievement, not because the working class lack an adequate culture but because the education system is essentially fixed in favour of people with upper- or middle-class backgrounds.

Pierre Bourdieu (1984) believes that your parents' possession (or lack) of one of four different types of capital can affect your achievement in the education system.

**Table 6**
Bourdieu: types of capital and education

| Definition | Example | Role in education |
|---|---|---|
| **Economic capital** | | |
| Ownership of wealth | Owning valuable houses, shares, having an income | Paying for private education or additional tuition |
| **Cultural capital** | | |
| Possession of educational qualifications, knowledge of arts and literature, and lifestyles, which are valued in society | Degree-level qualification or higher, educational holidays, knowledge of classic art and literature | Knowledge and experience to help children with school work. Educationally stimulating home environment – children become familiar with knowledge that is valued at school |
| **Social capital** | | |
| Possession of valuable social contacts | Knowing teachers, head-teachers, professors socially | May help with admission to best educational institutions or finding expert help |
| **Symbolic capital** | | |
| Possession of status | Having an image of respectability | Could help with admission to **private** or selective **schools** |

All these types of capital can help in education and all reflect class inequalities in society. However, cultural capital is particularly useful. The education system is biased towards the culture of higher social classes. Students from these classes therefore have an advantage because they have been socialized into the **dominant culture**.

### Essential notes

Bourdieu's ideas have been very influential. He was influenced by Marxist thinking (the dominant culture in society is reflected in the school **curriculum** and this helps those from higher or middle-class backgrounds), but he did not only discuss economic factors.

### Examiners' notes

This theory is essential in questions on class and differential achievement, as it helps to link factors inside and outside school. It can also be used to develop the Marxist theory in theory questions.

### Key study
### Stephen Ball et al.: Cultural capital and educational choice

Bourdieu's theory was supported in a study of parental choice in education by Ball et al. (2000). They looked at the process of choosing a secondary school and found that middle-class parents had a significant advantage over working-class parents.

- Middle-class parents have the knowledge and contacts to play the system to give their children the best chance of getting into the most successful schools (cultural and social capital).
- Working-class parents lacked the money to pay for transport to send their children to better but more distant schools, or to move into the **catchment area** of a successful school.
- Working-class parents were just as keen for their children to do well in education but they lacked the cultural capital and **material resources** to ensure success.

## Reay et al.: Social class and higher education

A study by Reay et al. found that cultural differences between classes affected choice of university. According to Bourdieu, each class has its own **habitus** (dispositions, tastes and lifestyle) and only feel comfortable in their own habitus. For example, working-class pupils often feel uncomfortable with applications to Oxford and Cambridge.

## Material factors and educational achievement

Despite the importance attached to culture by the above studies, they all see class inequalities based on material factors of wealth and income as the basis for the class divisions, which produce different cultures. However, material factors can directly cause class inequalities in educational achievement too.

### Material factors in schooling

Smith and Noble (1995) identify three ways in which affluence gives advantages to middle-class and upper-class pupils in the schooling system.

1. Having money makes it possible for parents to provide more books and educational toys, healthier diets, space to study in the home, computer facilities, private tuition and educational travel abroad.
2. Working-class parents cannot always afford school trips.
3. Schools in more affluent areas tend to be more successful and attract more pupils; this results in their getting more funding.

Britland (2013) argues that parents paying for private tutors gives some middle-class children a distinct advantage, while only the quite rich can afford to go to private schools.

### Material factors and higher education

Research by Reay et al. (2005) into higher education found that material factors, as well as cultural factors, were important. Affluent parents could pay for

- private tuition to help them get into the best universities
- financial support to attend universities in expensive cities
- help with living costs so children didn't have to work while studying.

Callender and Jackson (2004) found in survey research that worry about debt often put poorer students off going to university at all.

### Key study
### Hollingworth and Williams: Chavs, Charvers and Townies

Research by Hollingworth and Williams (2009) studied the **labelling** of working-class pupils by middle-class pupils in two schools, one in northern England and one in southern England. They interviewed families with parents and children together. Many subcultures were identified, but pupils seen as 'chavs, charvers or townies' were almost always working class. These terms were applied by middle-class pupils, not chosen by working-class pupils, and they were associated with negative stereotypes which might demotivate working-class pupils.

**Examiners' notes**

This study is also important in answering questions on policies because it shows how the market in education introduced by the New Right can be manipulated to benefit those from higher classes.

**Examiners' notes**

In 10-mark A-level questions, where you might have to outline and explain two effects of material inequality, you can include discussion of how much effect they have and how material factors interact with non-material ones. In 20- and 30-mark questions it will be important to contrast this type of explanation with cultural explanations and factors inside the education system.

**Examiners' notes**

Access to higher education is a topic of great contemporary relevance, given increases in student fees, so it is likely to impress the examiner if you can show knowledge of recent changes and apply it to a question.

**Examiners' notes**

You only need to discuss this background if asked specifically about the interactionist perspective.

## The interactionist perspective

Cultural deprivation and material explanations of differential educational achievement by social class both see factors outside the education system as responsible for class differences. The interactionist perspective, however, focuses on processes within schools and other educational institutions to explain differential achievement.

While interacting with others, people interpret and attach meanings to the behaviour of those around them. This affects people's image of themselves (**self-concept**), and self-concept in turn shapes behaviour. For example, if pupils are labelled as **deviants** or troublemakers their behaviour will tend to be seen as a deliberate attempt to cause trouble. The reaction of teachers will lead to the pupils also seeing themselves as deviants, and because of this they will tend to act in more deviant ways.

## Labelling

- According to the interactionist perspective, teachers may label pupils, or classify them into different types, and then act towards them on the basis of this classification.
- Hargreaves et al. (1975) found that factors such as a pupil's appearance, how they respond to discipline, how likeable they are and their personality, as well as whether they are deviant, leads to teachers attaching labels to them as 'good' or 'bad' pupils.
- Once given a label, teachers tend to interpret behaviour in terms of that label, and pupils tend to live up to the label.
- This results in a **self-fulfilling-prophecy,** in which the label results in the behaviour predicted by the teacher.
  1. Teacher forms impression of pupil.
  2. Pupil labelled as a troublemaker and teacher interprets behaviour as deviant.
  3. Pupil becomes aware of teacher's label.
  4. Pupil self-concept starts to change.
  5. Pupil starts living up to label.
  6. Initial label confirmed by behaviour; stronger labelling and more deviant behaviour occurs.

## Social class and labelling

Many interactionists claim that social class background affects the way that teachers label pupils. Middle-class pupils fit the teacher's **stereotype** of the **ideal pupil** better than working-class pupils, and therefore working-class pupils are more likely to be labelled as deviant or lazy.

Labelling can lead to pupils being placed in different ability groupings within school. Lower-class pupils may be more likely to be placed in lower **sets**, **bands** or **streams**. These lower groupings are likely to be seen as less able and as more likely to be disruptive. This can lead to the formation of pupil subcultures, with lower streams or sets more likely to form anti-school

**Examiners' notes**

This material is important for questions about processes within schools generally, not just questions on class and differential achievement.

subcultures. Among these pupils, academic work is not valued and **peer groups** encourage deviant behaviour and discourage hard work.

### Key study
### Mac an Ghaill: Labelling and peer groups

Máirtín Mac an Ghaill (1994) studied working-class students in a Midlands comprehensive school. The school had divided pupils into three sets and, as a result, three distinct, male, working-class peer groups developed:

- 'Macho lads' – academic failures who became hostile to the school and were usually from less skilled working-class backgrounds.
- 'Academic achievers' – academic 'successes', usually from more skilled working-class backgrounds, they tried hard at school.
- 'New enterprisers' – had a positive attitude to school and saw the vocational curriculum as a route to career success.

## Evaluation of interactionist approaches

Interactionist studies of education have certain advantages over other approaches:

- They are often based on detailed empirical evidence.
- They show that factors operating within school can have a significant impact on educational achievement.

However, they have been criticized as follows:

- They fail to explain where wider class inequalities come from.
- They ignore factors outside the school such as cultural and material factors, which may also affect achievement.
- They use simplified models of pupil subcultures and do not identify the full range of responses to school.
- Labelling theory sometimes sounds **deterministic**. Success and failure is entirely determined by the attitudes of teachers, giving pupils little apparent control over their own success.
- Not all pupils live up to labelling by teachers. A study by Margaret Fuller (1984) found that a group of black working-class girls who were labelled as likely failures responded by working harder to achieve success.

### Essential notes

This study demonstrates how class interacts with gender in shaping achievement.

### Examiners' notes

It is very important to emphasize that all the main types of inequality – class, gender and ethnicity – act together in shaping differential educational achievement. You can get analysis and evaluation marks for pointing this out, and then further marks if you back it up with reference to specific studies.

### Essential notes

Whatever the merits of these particular studies and the interactionist approach, there is little doubt that the nature of schools themselves plays some part in determining educational achievement. For example, some schools with a predominantly working-class intake do better than other schools with similar pupils. Overall, though, it is very difficult for the educational system to compensate for the inequalities in society as a whole.

## Ethnicity

- **Ethnic groups** are groups within a population regarded by themselves or others as culturally distinctive; they usually see themselves as having a common origin. Ethnicity may be linked to religion, nationality and other aspects of culture such as language and lifestyle.
- Largely as a result of **migration**, the UK has a number of distinctive ethnic groups. The largest minority ethnic groups in the UK are those of South Asian or African-Caribbean origin. The Irish and Chinese can also be regarded as minority ethnic groups.
- There are significant differences in educational achievement between ethnic groups, although the achievement gap between some ethnic groups has been narrowing.
- There are also differences in achievement between males and females within ethnic groups.

## Ethnic differences in achievement

One way of measuring educational achievement is by looking at the proportion of pupils gaining five or more GCSEs at grades A*–C. In 2014

- Chinese pupils had the highest proportion achieving this level (80.1% of girls and 70% of boys)
- followed by Asian pupils (64.9%)
- lowest levels of attainment were among black pupils (58.7%), while 60.4% of white pupils achieved this standard.

There are, however, major differences in achievement within broad ethnic groups. For example, children from Indian backgrounds do better than those from Pakistani backgrounds on average, and in all ethnic groups girls do better than boys.

## Changes over time

Over the past 20 years, minority ethnic groups have been gaining ground on white British people in the education system.

- In 1992, white British pupils were more than twice as likely as Bangladeshis to achieve five or more GCSEs at grades A*–C, but by 2006 Bangladeshis had overtaken white British pupils.
- By 2001–2, all minority ethnic groups had higher participation rates in higher education than white British people in England.
- Nevertheless, minority ethnic groups are still less likely to go to the more prestigious universities and, apart from Chinese and Indians, are less likely to attain a high-grade degree.

## Social class, ethnicity and achievement

Differences in achievement are partly the result of social class differences. Most minority ethnic groups are more likely to have working-class jobs than white British people. Since class has a major impact on levels of educational achievement, this partly explains underachievement by members of some minority ethnic groups.

However, government statistics suggest that class differences (when comparing pupils eligible for free school meals and those who are not) are greater among white British pupils than other ethnic groups (Haralambos and Holborn, 2013).

Modood (2004) argues that some ethnic minority pupils have higher levels of cultural capital, despite often being from a working-class background. For example, many Indians and East African Asians originate from working-class backgrounds even though they have middle-class jobs. The parents therefore may place a particularly high value on educational success and they have the knowledge and understanding of education to help their children to succeed.

## Cultural factors, ethnicity and achievement

Differences in educational achievements could also be the result of cultural factors such as the educational qualifications of parents and parental knowledge of, and interest in, the education system.

### Key study
### Strand: Ethnicity and achievement in secondary education

Strand (2007) compared the progress of Indian, African-Caribbean and white British pupils in the first four years of secondary school. Strand found that Indian children made more progress than white British children but African-Caribbean pupils fell further behind. The success of Indian pupils was due to both cultural and material factors such as

- high aspirations and dedication to homework
- low levels of truancy and exclusion
- good resource provision at home (such as computers or private tuition).

African-Caribbean pupils were held back mainly by material factors such as

- high levels of poverty
- living in poor accommodation
- attending schools in deprived areas.

There was no evidence, however, that African-Caribbean parents and pupils had a culture that would hold them back in education – they had high aspirations and a positive attitude to school. Overall the study found little difference in the cultural support for education between working-class white and African-Caribbean pupils, so it was difficult to explain why African-Caribbean pupils were doing less well.

## Family life, masculinity and underachievement

Tony Sewell (1997) claims that factors outside school explain the low achievement of many African-Caribbean boys. He argues:

- A high proportion of these boys are raised in lone-parent families headed by women.
- They therefore lack a positive adult male role model.

**Examiners' notes**

The interaction of class, gender and ethnicity is always useful in answers on differential achievement. Research suggests that class is the most important factor, so mention that class differences are bound to have an effect on ethnic differences in achievement. Class may affect some ethnic groups more than others, suggesting that the relationship is quite complex.

**Examiners' notes**

You always need to back up claims in this area with evidence from studies such as this. Otherwise you risk your answer seeming more like stereotypical comments about ethnic groups than good sociology.

☞ **This topic continues on the next two pages**

**Examiners' notes**

This is a useful study for essay questions because it allows you to discuss the point of view that sees factors outside school as being very important, when most studies put strong emphasis on factors inside school.

- This makes them vulnerable to peer pressure.
- They are more likely to be drawn into gangs, which emphasize macho masculinity.
- Gang culture compensates for a sense of rejection by fathers and the experience of racism in society and in school.
- Although most African-Caribbean boys try hard to succeed in school, a significant minority of about a quarter make little effort and form an anti-school culture or reject school in favour of street culture.

Sewell's arguments have been criticized by those who believe that he is blaming black culture for educational failure, when the real cause lies in racism within the education system, or society as a whole.

## Racism and educational underachievement

- Racism can be defined as negative beliefs or discriminatory behaviour directed at individuals or groups as a result of their 'race' or ethnicity.
- **Institutional racism** has been defined as 'the collective failure of an organization to provide an appropriate and professional service to people because of their colour, culture, or ethnic origin' (MacPherson, 1999).

**Examiners' notes**

The examiner will be impressed by appropriate use of the concept of institutional racism with an explanation of it, assuming, of course, that it is relevant.

A number of sociologists believe that the educational underachievement of some ethnic minorities, particularly African-Caribbean boys, is a result of racism, especially institutional racism.

This is reflected in school exclusion figures. In 2015, African-Caribbean pupils were about three times more likely to be excluded from school than the average in England and Wales (DfE, 2016).

African-Caribbean boys are particularly likely to be placed in lower sets.

Bernard Coard (1971) claimed that there was systematic racism in British education, with teachers having low expectations of black pupils, a curriculum that ignored black history and culture, and schools that tolerated casual racism in the playground.

These views are partly supported by some studies.

### Wright: Racism in primary schools

Cecile Wright (1992) conducted an ethnographic study of four multi-racial primary schools using observation and interviews with teachers. She found significant evidence of discrimination by teachers.

- Asian girls got less attention from teachers than other pupils, and their customs and traditions were sometimes met with hostility.
- African-Caribbean boys got plenty of attention from teachers, but nearly all of it was negative – teachers expected them to behave badly.

### Gillborn Mirza and Youdell: Rationing education

Gillborn et al. (2000) used documentary evidence about local education authorities, lesson observation and interviews with pupils and teachers in two London comprehensive schools.

They found evidence that some local authorities were particularly poor at educating ethnic minorities.

Within schools, they found a system of **educational triage**, in which education was rationed. Extra help was directed to pupils who were borderline for gaining five GCSEs at grades A*–C. Most black pupils were seen as having little chance of achieving this and so were not given extra help. Compared with white peers with similar levels of achievement, black pupils were placed in lower sets and entered for lower-tier exams.

There was also evidence of a system of racialized expectations. The behaviour of black pupils was often misinterpreted as threatening, when in reality it reflected a desire to take an active part in lessons and to succeed.

They conclude that unintentional racism based on misinterpretations holds back black pupils.

## Racism and the curriculum

Some sociologists argue that the curriculum neglects both ethnic minority culture and topics of specific interest to ethnic minorities. For example, geography and history tend to emphasize the positive benefits of British colonialism rather than the negative effects on the former colonies.

Tikly et al. (2006) studied 30 comprehensive schools and found that a large number of African-Caribbean pupils felt that their culture was invisible in the curriculum because of a white European focus. When black history was mentioned, it tended to be in relation to slavery rather than the positive contribution of black people to history.

## Conclusion

Inequality has been reduced, with most ethnic minority groups doing well in British education, but some significant problems remain, particularly for African-Caribbean boys.

The evidence suggests that factors inside and outside school combine to affect the performance of ethnic minorities in the education system.

- Unintentional racism in education probably plays some part in the **underachievement** of African-Caribbean pupils in particular.
- Some steps have been made to reduce unintentional racism, for example, through the introduction of a **multicultural curriculum.**
- Parental attitudes are probably not a factor, since research suggests parents from all ethnic groups are strongly interested in their children's education.
- Class inequality partially explains ethnic differences in achievement. It affects the educational achievements of all ethnic minorities, and has a particularly strong effect among white British, but little effect among Chinese and Indian pupils.
- Ethnicity interacts with class and gender to shape educational achievement, rather than acting independently of other social divisions.

**Examiners' notes**

You must refer to specific studies to have a good chance of getting into the top mark band in 20-mark and 30-mark questions on ethnicity and underachievement.

**Essential notes**

A useful study by Margaret Fuller (1984) found that some African-Caribbean girls worked extra hard and were determined to succeed despite experiencing racism in the education system.

**Essential notes**

Research by Heidi Mirza (1992) for her book *Young, Female and Black* found that many female black pupils had a positive self-image and could overcome the racism and stereotyping directed at them from a small minority of teachers, but sometimes well-meaning teachers were over-protective and failed to offer the sort of help the girls needed.

## Patterns of achievement

Historically, women have tended to achieve less well than men at higher levels in the British education system. Although girls always did better in the early years, until the early 1990s boys were more likely to gain A-level qualifications and to go on to study in higher education. Then, during the 1990s, girls overtook boys at all levels in the education system.

- In 2015, 53% of boys as opposed to 62% of girls gained five or more good (C grade or better) GCSEs including English and mathematics.
- In 2015, the average UCAS A-level points per entry was 213 for men but 225 for women.
- In 2014–15, 44% of students in higher education in England and Wales were male and 56% were female.
- Furthermore, on average, women now get better degrees than men. However, males do outperform females in some respects, for example, boys are more likely than girls to gain three or more A-levels at A or A* grades.

## Gender and subject choice

There continue to be significant differences in the choice of subjects by males and females. The National Curriculum has restricted subject choice at lower levels in the education system, but at A-level and degree level, and in vocational education, males and females still tend to choose different subjects.

At A-level:
- Boys are more likely to do business studies, economics, politics, sciences (apart from biology), technical subjects and politics.
- Girls are more likely to do all other subjects and for English, modern languages, psychology and sociology they are the big majority of candidates.

At degree level:
- Men are more likely to graduate in physical sciences, maths, engineering, technology, architecture, building and planning.
- Women are more likely to graduate in all other subjects and have overtaken males in medicine, dentistry and business and financial studies.

## Feminist perspectives on education: Female underachievement and gendered curriculum choice

Despite the relative success of females in the education system, feminists have identified ways in which females may have been disadvantaged. Feminists generally believe that the education system is **patriarchal** or male-dominated. Although feminist perspectives may be more relevant to previous decades, some of the processes may still prevent females from achieving their full potential within education. There are also some areas where women still seem to be at a disadvantage.

- The feminist Miriam David (2008) points out that women are proportionately more likely to attend new, post-1992 universities than more prestigious institutions.

- Female disadvantage may still have an effect on subject choices, and particularly the under-representation of women in most science subjects.

## Key study
## Classroom behaviour

The feminist Michelle Stanworth (1983) studied A-level classes in a further education college. She found the following bias against girls:

- Teachers found it more difficult to remember the girls in their class.
- Teachers did not expect even the most able girls to go into high-status jobs.
- Pupils believed that boys received more attention than girls, and boys were more likely to join in classroom discussion and to be asked questions by the teachers.
- Girls underestimated their own ability.

Stanworth's research has been criticized by Randall (1987) for being based on interviews rather than direct observation of classroom interaction. Randall's own research failed to find the same bias against girls.

### Essential notes

Despite its age, this is a useful study for illustrating many of the basic points made by feminists. As the more recent research by Francis shows, classroom interaction may still be male-dominated.

### Francis: Girls and achievement

Some more recent studies by Francis (2000) do suggest that there continues to be some disadvantages for girls in the education system.

- Research in London schools found that males still dominate classrooms.
- Boys are disciplined more frequently and more harshly than girls, but this leads to girls getting less attention than boys.
- Gender divisions in subject choice are getting stronger, with fewer women taking IT and pure science degrees.

### Colley: Gender inequalities in subject choice

Colley (1998) explains the continuing differences in subject choice by gender in the following way:

- Traditional definitions of masculinity and **femininity** are still widespread.
- Subjects continue to have different images; for example, computer studies, which involves working with machines rather than people and offers little opportunity for group activities, still retains a masculine image.
- Girls tend to feel comfortable with scientific and technical subjects only when taught in single-sex schools or single-sex classes.

### Socialization

Norman et al. (1988) argue that **sex stereotyping** starts from a very young age. For example:

- Girls are given dolls and other toys that emphasize a caring role; this can affect career aspirations and subject choice.

### Examiners' notes

These points could form the basis of a 4-mark or 6-mark AS question, a 6-mark A-level question, or two of them could be developed further in response to 10-mark questions for either exam.

### Essential notes

A 2012 report for The Institute of Physics found that a lack of role models, such as female physicists on TV, and a shortage of physics teachers (meaning that it was not always offered in all-female sixth forms) helped explain why so few girls took physics. In addition, boys still dominated many physics classrooms in coeducational schools.

☞ This topic continues on the next two pages

**Essential notes**

Skelton et al. (2007) believe that these types of factor end up producing different conceptions of what is considered 'normal' for boys and girls in educational contexts (and beyond), and this is deeply embedded in the way educational institutions work.

- Boys are more likely to be given constructional toys and other toys that help to develop scientific and mathematical skills and concepts.
- Gender stereotypes are continually reinforced through the media.

**Feminist perspectives: Conclusion**

Radical feminists continue to argue that society as a whole is male-dominated or patriarchal.

Liberal feminists also think that society is patriarchal to an extent, but they do accept that important changes have taken place, so that the inequality between men and women has declined.

Since females now do better than males in most aspects of the education system, there is little support for radical feminist perspectives in the evidence about changes in the education system.

**Liberal feminism** is on stronger ground in arguing that there are still some ways in which women and girls lose out in the education system. Boys still do better than girls in some of the more prestigious subjects and are more likely to gain entry to more prestigious universities. It is also possible that there continue to be disadvantages for girls and women, which prevent them from doing even better than they do now. **Gender roles** in society and **gender socialization** still seem to have an impact on subject choice and aspirations, although to a much lesser extent than in the past.

## Reasons for improvements in girls' achievement

The performance of girls in education has improved in absolute terms – they achieve more and get higher qualifications. Also, in relative terms, they have overtaken boys. A variety of explanations have been put forward for this change.

### Changes in the labour market

Opportunities for women in the labour market have greatly improved, creating more incentive for women to succeed in education.

The proportion of women of working age in employment has risen from approximately 50% in 1960 to more than 75%. There has been an expansion of **service sector** jobs, which are seen as more suitable for women, and a contraction of manual jobs and jobs in manufacturing, regarded as more suitable for men.

Francis and Skelton (2005) found that jobs with a predominantly female workforce increasingly require degree-level qualifications (for example, nursing, teaching and occupational therapy). This provides incentives for women to continue in post-compulsory education.

### Changes in women's aspirations

A number of changes have affected the aspirations of women and made them more likely to aspire to high educational qualifications.

## Key study
## Sue Sharpe: Girls' aspirations

Sue Sharpe (1976, 1994) interviewed a sample of girls in the 1970s and a similar sample in the 1990s. She found that over this time their priorities had changed. In the 70s, love and marriage were their first priority, but by the 90s, jobs and careers were top of the list, with love and marriage seen as less important. This is reflected in more recent research by Rampino and Taylor (2013), which found that girls have higher aspirations than boys.

### Examiners' notes

This is a straightforward study, which makes an important point. It is also potentially useful for discussing the use of interviews in studying education.

Francis and Skelton (2005) found that middle-class parents are increasingly concerned about the educational success of their daughters and no longer prioritize the educational achievement of sons.

Mitsos and Browne (1998) believe that the women's movement and feminism have raised the aspirations, expectations and self-esteem of women, so that they aspire to professional and managerial jobs and to achieving qualifications that will enable them to get such jobs.

### Essential notes

One example of this is parents being more willing to pay for private education for their daughters than they were in the past.

## Socialization for schooling

- Evidence suggests that girls are putting more effort into homework and taking education more seriously than boys.
- Research by Burns and Bracey (2001) has found that girls are better organized and more willing to draft and redraft assignments. They also found that girls tend to read more than boys. This helps them to succeed in subjects requiring the use of language.

## Changes in education

Feminist research in the 1980s helped to increase awareness of possible gender bias against girls in the education system and has made educational institutions more aware of the need to provide equal opportunities for girls.

The introduction of the National Curriculum removed any tendency for girls to be denied access to academic subjects previously only made available to boys.

- Pirie (2001) believes that the shift towards coursework has benefited girls at the expense of boys. Research suggests that boys tend to cram for exams quite effectively but are poor at organizing themselves to be successful at coursework.
- However, research by Myhill (1999) raises questions, since the increase in the use of unseen exams in English has been accompanied by a more rapid improvement in girls' performance than that of boys.

It remains to be seen whether a recent move away from coursework will narrow the **gender gap**.

## Reasons for improvement in girls' achievement: Conclusion

As well as the above factors, the relative improvement of females in education could partly be explained by the relative decline of males, which is discussed in the next section.

## Boys' underachievement in perspective

The relative **underachievement** of boys in the education system has been a matter of increasing concern. However, boys' performance in education has in fact been improving, but just not as quickly as that of girls. Francis and Skelton (2005) believe that concern over this issue has been an exaggerated '**moral panic**' – a sudden and illogical outburst about a supposed decline in society that does not reflect reality.

However:

- There is evidence that certain boys are underachieving. Working-class boys still tend to do very poorly in the education system.
- There has been a widening of the gender gap – the difference in performance between men and women.

This suggests that there is some problem to explain.

## Changes in the labour market

Although women have benefited from changes in the labour market, in comparison, men have tended to become disadvantaged.

- A decline in manufacturing industry has led to a reduction in the **availability** of manual jobs, which are predominantly done by men.
- There has been a rise in the proportion of service sector jobs, which are predominantly done by women.
- An increase in part-time and temporary jobs may be more suited to women, who combine childcare with paid work, than to men seeking full-time employment in order to act as the primary **breadwinner** in a household.
- An increase in long-term unemployment tends to affect men more than women.

All of the above may reduce the motivation of working-class boys in particular, who may see little likelihood of occupational success. The decline or disappearance of some of the roles, which in the past defined being masculine – such as being a breadwinner or doing a manual job – is sometimes described as part of a **crisis in masculinity**.

## Boys in the education system

A variety of research suggests that the relative lack of success of boys stems from the interaction between the culture of masculinity and the education system.

Research by Francis (2000) suggests that both genders face problems in education, but there are a number of problems specific to boys. These are:

1. Boys get more classroom attention from teachers but are criticized more by teachers than girls. This can demotivate them and lower their expectations.
2. Changing teacher attitudes and publicity about male underachievement have led to boys losing their confidence.
3. The stereotype of the ideal pupil tends to fit girls better than boys. Girls may seem more organized and be more conscientious than

boys. If boys are labelled as a problem, this can lead to a self-fulfilling prophecy where their behaviour becomes worse and their achievement declines.

4. Boys are generally keen to remain popular with their **peer group** and do not wish to risk being known as 'swots', 'nerds' or 'geeks' by being seen to work too hard at school.

### Key study
### Jackson: Laddish culture

Jackson (2006) used interviews and questionnaires to study masculinity and femininity in eight schools. She found:

- The schools were dominated by a culture of **hegemonic** (or dominant) masculinity which valued toughness, power and competitiveness.
- Academic work was seen as being essentially feminine and therefore 'uncool' by boys.
- Boys tended to mess around to impress their peer group rather than concentrating on the work – acting out a culture of laddish masculinity.
- Some boys did want to succeed but, to avoid being seen as 'uncool', worked mainly at home. This disadvantaged working-class boys who had poorer facilities at home; for example, less space to study or limited access to a computer or the internet.
- Working-class boys were particularly affected by changes in the labour market. Lacking the prospect of employment to give them a sense of identity, laddish behaviour was used to restore a sense of masculine pride.

### Examiners' notes

The interaction of laddish culture with what happens inside the education system seems to be very important and needs discussing in any longer answers on this topic.

Other factors operating inside the education system are identified by Mitsos and Browne (1998). They argue that:

- Teachers now have low expectations of boys. They expect them to be disruptive and their work to be late and rushed. They therefore tend not to push boys to do better when they are underperforming.
- Boys may become disillusioned with education in their early years. Primary school environments tend to be female-dominated and may have an excessive emphasis on being neat and tidy, which are not boys' strengths.

## Conclusion

Feminists such as Osler (2006) believe that the current concern about underachievement by boys has led to a neglect of the problem of underachievement among girls. For example, when pupils are excluded from school more help is now available for boys than for girls.

The emphasis on underachievement by boys could also obscure the importance of social class, since it is largely working-class boys who underachieve.

### Examiners' notes

You could structure a 20- or 30-mark answer around the contrasting views of feminists and those who do see male underachievement as a serious problem. As well as theory, you can then include analysis and balanced evaluation.

## Introduction

The **formal curriculum** involves the subjects, which are on the school timetable, such as English, history and physics. The hidden curriculum exists alongside this formal curriculum and involves the hidden, informal messages and lessons that come from the way schooling is organized and run. These messages are reflected in the overall ethos of the school, which in turn influences the kinds of behaviours and attitudes that are valued and rewarded and also those, which are looked down on and can lead to punishment.

## Examiners' notes

You could be asked to define aspects of the hidden curriculum for 2 marks or to give three ways in which the hidden curriculum operates for 6 marks.

| Example | Hidden message/value |
|---------|---------------------|
| The school is based on a hierarchy with the headteacher having most power and pupils having very little power | People should not expect to have much control over their own lives but should accept direction from above |
| Men hold most senior positions in a school, while most cleaners are women | It is normal for men to be dominant in society |
| Pupils are rewarded for punctuality and punished for being late | Conformity to strict rules is valued above other attributes |

**Table 7**
Examples of the hidden curriculum

Some perspectives are critical of the hidden curriculum, while others see it as an invaluable and integral part of schooling.

## Functionalism and the hidden curriculum

As discussed on page 4, functionalists believe that education teaches attitudes and values, which are beneficial to society as a whole. These values help society to function smoothly and education helps to integrate members into society.

According to Durkheim (1961), school teaches

- a sense of belonging and commitment to a bigger society
- a shared belief in the importance of cooperation
- school assemblies, team games and anything that produces a sense of pride in a pupil's individual school helps to pass on these values.

According to Parsons (1961) school teaches:

- a belief that individual achievement should be based on merit
- a belief in individual competition through which individuals learn to make the maximum possible contribution to society.

The exam system plays a particularly important role in this.

## Marxism and the hidden curriculum

Marxists criticize functionalists by arguing that the hidden curriculum benefits the ruling class and not society as a whole.

### Key study
### Bowles and Gintis: Capitalism and the hidden curriculum

As discussed on page 7, the Marxists Bowles and Gintis (1976) believe that the main role of the hidden curriculum is to produce a docile, easily manipulated and exploitable workforce for capitalists. This is achieved in the following ways:

- High grades are awarded to pupils who conform rather than those who think critically and creatively.
- Schools are based on a hierarchy in which pupils obey teachers. This gets them accustomed to the obedience that will be necessary towards managers.
- School teaches that you should not expect to feel fulfilled in your daily activities. School is boring and this is preparation for work in capitalism, which is also boring and **alienating**.
- You are taught instead to be motivated by external rewards such as exam success or a pay packet.
- Rather than teaching a sense of commitment to a social group, school divides pupils, as they compete with one another. This prevents the collectivist outlook that is important for the development of trade unions.

## Feminism and the hidden curriculum

Feminists agree with Marxists that the hidden curriculum does not serve the interests of society as a whole, but instead benefits a particular group. However, unlike Marxists, they see the hidden curriculum as promoting patriarchal values that ensure the dominance of men in society.

Michelle Stanworth (1983) found that education gave the following messages to women:

- Men are more important than women.
- Boys' careers are more important than girls' careers. (Teachers encouraged boys more than girls in pursuing careers.)
- Boys are cleverer than girls.
- Senior positions in education are disproportionately held by men. This reinforces the message that males are and should be dominant.

## The hidden curriculum: Evaluation

There is no doubt that schools have a hidden curriculum, but how consistent this is and how far it is accepted by pupils is more open to debate.

- Neo-Marxists such as Giroux (1984) see schools as sites of ideological struggle. A variety of groups compete to influence education and they do not always share the same values.
- Paul Willis (1977) points out that many pupils do not accept the values promoted by the school and some rebel completely against those values by forming **anti-school subcultures**.
- Individual perspectives tend to generalize about the hidden curriculum of schools. For example, some schools and individual teachers may actively promote equality between the sexes and therefore not support a patriarchal hidden curriculum.

### Examiners' notes

In 20- or 30-mark questions, comparing and contrasting the views of different perspectives on the hidden curriculum is an excellent way to demonstrate the analytical and evaluative skills necessary to get into the top mark band.

### Essential notes

Additional evaluation of this study can be found on page 7.

### Essential notes

Subject choice may reflect a hidden curriculum that portrays some subjects as being more masculine and others as being more feminine. The sex of teachers of different subjects, whether males or females are depicted in textbooks or even if (supposedly more feminine) group work is included in classroom teaching, are all influences.

### Examiners' notes

These points are valuable for including evaluation and balance in any 20- or 30-mark answers on this topic.

## Subcultures

A subculture is a group within a wider culture, which to some extent has distinctive attitudes, values, norms or lifestyles from the wider culture within which it is embedded.

If a school as a whole can be seen as having one dominant culture with its own distinct ethos, then subcultures are groups to which a minority belong and which differ significantly from the dominant culture. All subcultures encourage loyalty and the sense of identity from members of the subculture. In return, members are given status by their peers within the group.

Hargreaves (1967) believed that the main reason that subcultures form is so that pupils who receive little status within the school as a whole can gain status by forming or belonging to a subculture in which they are valued. He found that lower-stream boys tended to form their own subcultures in which they could get status for defying school rules and opposing its culture.

## The basis of subculture formation

Subcultures can be partly or wholly based on a number of social divisions that exist either in the wider society or within schools. These can include:

- Class background – working-class and middle-class pupils may form different subcultures
- Gender – both male and female subcultures
- Ethnicity – Asian, African-Caribbean or white subcultures
- Sets or streams – higher and lower sets or streams often have distinctive subcultures
- Youth culture – for example, a distinctive 'goth' subculture within a school
- Sexuality – gay and straight subcultures

Often a combination of these factors all work together; for example, when a subculture is dominated by white, working-class, male pupils.

## Male subcultures

Many studies have concentrated on anti-school subcultures, which have been formed by academic failures who have become hostile to a school because they gain little status from teachers.

For example, Willis (1977) distinguished the anti-school 'lads' and the pro-school 'ear' 'oles'. The 'lads' were white, working-class, male and in the lower streams, whereas the 'ear' 'oles' were generally middle class. Willis therefore identified a clear dichotomy between two opposite subcultures. Other sociologists, however, have identified more complex subcultural divisions.

> **Key study**
>
> **Mac an Ghaill: The variety of male subcultures**
>
> Máirtín Mac an Ghaill (1994), in a study of boys in secondary education, identified five distinct subcultures:
>
> 1. 'Academic achievers' – bought into the idea of being upwardly mobile through working hard.

**Examiners' notes**

Look out for 6- or 10-mark questions about types of subcultures or reasons why subcultures form.

**Examiners' notes**

Emphasize that Willis believed that class divisions in the wider society led to the formation of subcultures, and that processes within school reflected these wider structures.

2. 'Macho lads' – opposed to the values of the school and the authority of teachers and saw the academic achievers as effeminate.
3. 'New enterprisers' – were pro-school but were keener on vocational education as a path to success.
4. 'Real Englishman' – a small group of mainly middle-class pupils from highly educated backgrounds who valued education for its own sake.
5. Gay students – critical of the homophobia of school.

## Female subcultures

Most studies have concentrated on male subcultures within schools, but there have also been some studies of female subcultures. Griffin (1985) found that girls were less likely than boys to form larger subcultures. Her research suggested that girls were more likely to form small friendship groups.

### Scott Davies: Exaggerated femininity

Scott Davies (1995), in a Canadian study, did find evidence of anti-school female subcultures. The members had an exaggerated sexuality – emphasizing boyfriends and prioritizing marriage and childbearing over academic success.

## Ethnicity and subcultures

Some studies have found a tendency for male African-Caribbean pupils to form anti-school subcultures because they may suffer racism, tend to be placed in lower streams and are more likely to be excluded from school than their white counterparts. However, research by Sewell (1997) suggests a more complex picture.

### Key study

### Tony Sewell: African-Caribbean subcultures

In a study of an all-boys school, Sewell found the following subcultures:

1. Conformists – accepted the values of the school and tried to succeed through education.
2. Innovators – wanted to succeed but disliked the process of schooling. They did not seek approval from teachers but they did try to keep themselves out of trouble.
3. Retreatists – individuals who tended to keep themselves to themselves and didn't join the other subcultures.
4. Rebels – strongly rejected the school, and were aggressively masculine.

## Conclusion

- A variety of factors can form the basis for subcultures and there can be a variety of subcultures within any school.
- Not all individual pupils belong to a subculture.
- Academic success and attitudes towards it form an important element in defining different types of subculture, whether based on class, ethnicity or gender.

**Examiners' notes**

Use this study to illustrate the point that subcultures are not necessarily either entirely pro or anti the dominant culture of schools. Include extra analysis and evaluation to help you get into the top band.

**Examiners' notes**

Include some discussion of female subcultures for a balanced answer.

**Essential notes**

Pages 21–22 include a detailed explanation of the factors outside education which Sewell believes leads to the formation of these subcultures. However, his research has its critics who argue that racism within schools is much more important.

## Teacher expectations

There is a good deal of research that suggests that teachers tend to classify or **label** pupils, often on the basis of limited information.

As discussed on pages 18–19 interactionist theory suggests that a label, which defines someone as a particular type of person can affect a person's perception of themselves, or their **self-concept**. This in turn can shape a person's behaviour and result in a self-fulfilling prophecy. When a teacher predicts that a pupil will do well or poorly, they communicate this belief to the pupil in some way; this affects the self-concept of the pupil and the pupil lives up to the expectations of the teacher.

### Key study

### Rosenthal and Jacobson: The self-fulfilling prophecy

In a famous study, Rosenthal and Jacobson (1968) tested the theory of the self-fulfilling prophecy using a **field experiment**. In a state primary school in California, they gave teachers false information about the IQ scores of some of the pupils. Pupils were selected at random but teachers were informed that one group was particularly bright and were expected to do very well, while another group had low IQ scores and were expected to make little progress. The study found that, in general, the pupils performed in line with the information that had been given to the teachers. Regardless of their actual IQ scores, the pupils that the teachers had been told were intelligent made much more progress than those whom they believed had low intelligence.

A large number of attempts have been made to **replicate** this research and to test the results. However, while some of these studies have found evidence to support Rosenthal and Jacobson, many have not found evidence that labelling produces a significant effect.

## The ideal pupil and ability

Relationships between teachers and pupils can be shaped by teachers' conceptions of the ideal pupil.

- Research suggests that teachers see the ideal pupil as one who conforms to **middle-class** standards of behaviour – those who are cooperative and hard-working, polite and unlikely to challenge the teacher.
- The ideal pupil is also seen as one who clearly has ability, that is, the potential to do well.
- Research by Gillborn and Youdell (2001) has found that when judging pupils, teachers tend to see ability as fixed. They therefore tend to believe that some pupils have limited potential.
- Gillborn and Youdell found in their research that middle-class and white pupils were much more likely than other pupils to fit the image of the ideal pupil, and therefore to be seen as having high ability.

- Pupils who did not fit the ideal were more likely to have their behaviour judged negatively, and to be placed in lower sets or to be excluded from school.
- This led to poor relationships between teachers and some ethnic minority pupils. In particular, it led to hostility from some African-Caribbean boys.

## The organization of teaching and learning

As discussed on page 18, the allocation of pupils to different groups can have an effect on educational progress. The main ways of organizing pupils into different groups are as follows:

1. **mixed ability** – groups where pupils of all abilities are taught together in a single class
2. **streaming** – pupils taught in separate groups for all subjects, based on what is believed to be their overall ability level
3. **setting** – pupils are placed in particular groups according to their perceived ability in specific subjects
4. **within-class groupings** – pupils placed in different groups; for example, on different tables within a class, and given different work to do.

All ways of allocating pupils to different groups can affect the self-concept of individuals and their level of confidence.

Research by Gillborn et al. (2000) found that black pupils were often placed in lower sets, even when they had demonstrated as much ability as some white pupils placed in higher sets (see p 22).

> **Key study**
>
> **Hallam et al.: Teaching and learning in primary schools**
>
> Hallam et al. (2004) studied six primary schools with different ways of organizing teaching and learning. This included those that used mixed ability and others that used streaming.
>
> They found that:
>
> - Most pupils preferred whole-class or individual work rather than having within-class groupings, as they disliked feeling left out.
> - Children in mixed ability groups were better adjusted and had better attitudes to peers than those in streamed schools.
> - Negative attitudes to those in the lower streams were common, and pupils in lower streams often had fewer friends than those in high streams.
>
> In a review of research into secondary schooling, Hallam et al. found evidence that streaming played a major role in creating pro- and anti-school subcultures. Also, on balance, they found that setting seems to have a negative impact on performance in maths.

## Conclusion

Research suggests that different ways of organizing schooling does not have much impact on overall results, but it does tend to create greater inequality between the performance of more able and less able pupils.

## The start of state education

Before 1870, some elementary education was provided by churches and charities, and children could attend fee-paying **public schools** or selective grammar schools for secondary education. A third of children received no education at all.

In 1870 the Education Act provided state schools for all five to 11-year-olds and, in 1880, state education was made compulsory up to the age of 10.

In 1902 Local Education Authorities (**LEAs**) were established and the number of grammar schools was expanded. Although grammar schools still charged fees, some **working-class** children who passed a scholarship exam were given free education.

## The 1944 Education Act

In 1944 state education was completely reorganized, with the intention of providing a comprehensive and free education for everybody up to the age of 15.

The 1944 Act established three types of secondary school under the **tripartite system**, as shown in **Table 8**. This was based on the assumption that different types of pupil were better suited to different types of education. The differences were based on what was seen to be an innate ability, which was believed to be fixed and measurable at the age of 11, using intelligence tests or **IQ tests**.

The IQ test given to pupils was known as the 11+. It consisted of questions that were supposed to measure the abstract reasoning ability of pupils.

## Essential notes

Functionalists link the expansion of education to the requirement of industrial societies for more skilled workers in a more complex division of labour.

## Essential notes

Some of the research supporting the view that intelligence is innate and can be measured in IQ tests was conducted by Sir Cyril Burt. His work was later discredited when it was discovered that he had falsified some of the data.

## Examiners' notes

Only include a discussion of these policies if the question asks you to go this far back in time. If it asks about policies in the last 30 years, the tripartite system is not relevant.

| Type of institution | Basis of admission | Type of education | Typical pupils |
|---|---|---|---|
| Grammar school | Passing an IQ test (the 11+). Provided for around 20% of pupils | Academic education – often included classics | Mainly middle-class. In some areas, more places for boys than girls |
| Secondary modern school | Failing 11+ and lacking aptitude in technical subjects. Provided for around 75% of pupils | Less academic than grammar schools, much more emphasis on practical and vocational subjects | Mainly working-class |
| Technical school | Aptitude for technical subjects. Provided for around 5% of pupils | Emphasizing technical, vocational skills | Variety of backgrounds, particularly skilled working-class; more boys than girls |

**Table 8**
The tripartite system

## Criticisms of the tripartite system

1. Many critics argued that the 11+ did not truly measure ability. It was also argued that 11 was too young to measure ability.
2. The different types of school were not regarded as having equal status.
3. Fewer places were provided in grammar schools for girls than boys, even though girls tended to score higher in the 11+ exam.
4. From a social democratic perspective (see p 10), the system was socially divisive, since grammar schools were predominantly middle class and secondary moderns predominantly working class.

## The introduction of comprehensives

Partly because of the criticisms put forward by social democrats, comprehensive schools started to be introduced in the 1960s.

Comprehensive schools were intended to

1. break down class divisions by ensuring that people from all classes were educated in the same sort of school
2. create more **equal opportunities**, since no one would be disadvantaged by being sent to second-class schools.

## Evaluation of comprehensives

The introduction of comprehensives was controversial and some critics, particularly Conservative Party supporters, argued that they were ineffective. Their objections were:

1. Comprehensives lowered standards by undermining the excellent academic education offered in grammar schools. The most able did not have their ability stretched and the poor behaviour of the less able dragged down those who wanted to work hard and succeed.
2. Comprehensives had poor discipline, which made progress for all children problematic.
3. They were less successful than grammar schools in offering academic education which stretched talented working-class children and which facilitated **upward social mobility**.

Some supporters of social democratic policies also felt that comprehensives were a failure: the introduction of **streaming** and **setting** reproduced academic and class divisions within the schools. The higher academic sets were generally middle class, while the non-academic, lower sets were mainly working class.

However, there is some evidence that comprehensives did not lead to a lowering of standards. For example, the proportion of the population gaining A-levels and higher grade O-levels (now GCSEs) increased.

**Examiners' notes**

If you are answering essay questions on the development of policy, link these criticisms to the social democratic perspective and continuing political debates about the best way to organize education.

**Examiners' notes**

In 2016, an annex was opened to an existing grammar school in a different town, and the idea of allowing new grammar schools to be opened was being discussed, making these issues relevant to contemporary education.

**Examiners' notes**

You will not get a specific question on comprehensives, but the arguments are useful for discussing later policies of parental choice, marketization and the introduction of academies; policies designed to overcome the supposed deficiencies of comprehensives.

This topic continues on the next two pages

## The Conservatives and the New Right

As discussed on page 10, the neoliberals (also sometimes called the New Right or **market liberals**) believe that state-run services tend to be inefficient. They argue that a free market, in which companies compete for business, provides incentives for improvement in the quality of services over time. Expenditure by the state that they see as unnecessary or excessive is a drain on the economy, since it must be paid for out of taxes that ultimately come from the profits of companies.

They believe that the introduction of market forces, competition and choice into education can lead to greater **efficiency** and improve standards by creating a more skilled workforce. They are therefore in favour of the **marketization** of education – creating a market in education, just as there is a market for the products of private businesses.

Neoliberals were not in favour of making all pupils attend comprehensive schools since this limited choice, restricted competition and, in their view, lowered standards and undermined academic education. They were in favour of a greater emphasis on vocational education for pupils who were not academic so that they would leave education with the skills required by employers. To neoliberals, the purpose of education was to promote economic growth by raising standards and training the workforce, rather than to try to produce greater equality or eradicate class differences.

## Neoliberal educational reform

The Conservative governments of Margaret Thatcher and John Major (1979 to 1997) were strongly influenced by neoliberal philosophy.

Significant reforms in schooling were introduced in the 1988 Education Reform Act. **Table 9** summarizes the main provisions of this Act.

| Policy | Details of policy | Purpose of policy | Problems/criticisms |
|---|---|---|---|
| Formula funding and open enrolment | School admissions were not controlled by Local Education Authorities (LEAs) and schools could enrol as many pupils as they could physically fit into the buildings. Parents given more choice of school. Funding based on the number of pupils attracted | Competition would drive up standards. Popular schools could expand, so more pupils got a good education. Poorer schools had to improve or teachers' jobs were at risk | Schools in middle-class areas tended to be better than those in working-class areas. Popular schools tended to be oversubscribed, so many people did not get their first choice. Middle classes manipulated the system to their advantage |

| Policy | Details of policy | Purpose of policy | Problems/criticisms |
|---|---|---|---|
| National Curriculum | The government stipulates most of the curriculum content, with detailed targets for achievement of pupils at different key stages | To ensure that basic skills (e.g. English, maths and science) are taught consistently, so school leavers are employable. To provide a common basis for measuring progress and evaluating school performance | The National Curriculum restricted choice of subjects designed to meet local needs/interests. Some saw a cultural bias in the content, (e.g. a lack of concern with issues of interest to minority ethnic groups) |
| Testing and attainment targets | Performance tests introduced at ages seven, 11, 14 and 16 | To provide information at all levels of school education and to focus the efforts of schools on achieving key targets | Amount of testing seen to be excessive and led to schools focusing too much on tests |
| Introduction of league tables and regular, published inspections | League tables were introduced to judge the performance of schools. School inspections became more frequent and the reports more easily accessible to parents | To provide information to parents so that they could make rational decisions about choice of school. To make schools more accountable and therefore drive up standards | Schools that can attract more able pupils have a built-in advantage. League tables measure a limited range of outcomes and schools focus on achieving league table success rather than broader educational objectives |
| Introduction of new types of school | Existing schools could become grant-maintained – funded directly by government rather than the local education authority. **City Technology Colleges**, situated in inner cities, were partly funded by the private sector. They emphasized maths, science and technology | Intended to provide more choice and greater variety in the education system, to encourage further competition | Grant-maintained schools were a way of reintroducing selection, which mainly benefited the middle class. Seen as designed to reduce the power of Labour-run councils as much as to improve education |

**Table 9**
The Education Reform Act, 1988

## Examiners' notes

You may need to describe particular policies to answer 4-, 6-, 10-, 20- or 30-mark questions. Many of these policies are still broadly being followed, so evaluation remains relevant for discussing contemporary policies in longer questions.

### Examiners' notes

This is a useful study for evaluating the policies of all recent governments promoting competition within education. Reference to specific research can help you get into the top mark band on 10-, 20- and 30-mark questions by adding depth to the analysis and evaluation.

### Key study

#### Stephen Ball et al.: Educational choice and markets

Stephen Ball et al. (1994) conducted studies of the effects of the educational reforms introduced by Margaret Thatcher's Conservative government. They found that some groups took more advantage of the introduction of markets than others.

- Middle-class parents were usually **privileged/skilled choosers**. They had the time and social contacts to make informed choices about which were the best schools. Many had the money to move home to be in the catchment area for the most successful state schools or to pay for private education if necessary.
- Working-class parents were usually **disconnected choosers**. With limited access to private transport, they often chose the local school and based decisions on the happiness of their children rather than the academic reputation of the school.

The new policies had a number of negative effects on the education system.

- All schools tried hard to attract the most academically able students to boost league table results.
- Less attention was paid to students with special educational needs.
- Time and resources were devoted to improving school image to attract pupils.
- Cooperation between neighbouring schools became less common.
- Most schools tried to portray a traditional academic image; for example, by enforcing rules about school uniform, so there was little real choice for parents.

## Evaluation of marketization in schooling

Critics of the reforms argue that they reintroduced and strengthened class divisions within the education system.

### Essential notes

Cream-skimming has also become possible with the introduction of specialist schools (under New Labour), and **academies** and **free schools** under the coalition and post-2015 Conservative government.

Bartlett and Le Grand (1993) see the system as resulting in **cream-skimming** – the most successful schools in the wealthiest areas are able to attract the most able students from the most affluent backgrounds. As schools increasingly set their own selection criteria, they could find ways to choose 'respectable' and hard-working pupils for their schools; for example, by insisting that applicants have regularly attended a religious institution. Schools started to choose parents rather than parents choosing schools.

## New vocationalism

New vocationalism involved a renewed emphasis on training individuals for particular jobs or vocations. Neoliberals believed that many school leavers were unemployable and this was restricting Britain's economic growth. Education had become too dominated by the beliefs of left-wing educational professionals, and employers had too little input into the content of education. A number of measures were introduced.

- YTS (the Youth Training Scheme) – a two-year course that combined work experience with education. It was aimed at unemployed young people who were thought to lack basic skills. Employers were paid to take, and train, unemployed youths.
- NVQs (National Vocational Qualifications) – qualifications that laid down standards in particular occupations. These were often studied part-time in colleges while students worked in the occupation.
- GNVQs (General National Vocational Qualifications) – broader alternatives to academic courses that prepared pupils for work in a general occupational area such as leisure and tourism.
- Modern apprenticeships – combined work-based training with attendance at college to help young workers achieve NVQ qualifications.

## Criticisms of new vocationalism

Phil Cohen (1984) saw the real purpose of vocational training as the creation of attitudes that made young people easily exploited workers. If they did not join training schemes and conform to the requirements of the schemes, they were disciplined by the threat of having benefits removed. The skills taught were only suitable for very low-paid and low-skilled jobs.

Dan Finn (1987) criticized training schemes for offering cheap labour for employers, who provided little real training. He believed the real purpose was to manipulate unemployment statistics by taking people off the register and also to undermine trade union power, since trainees were unlikely to be members of unions. Finn denied that school leavers were unemployable, since most had already worked part-time. The real problem was simply a lack of jobs in the economy.

## Conclusion

Although various aspects of the reforms introduced by neoliberal governments were heavily criticized, many of them were retained when a New Labour government was elected in 1997. Some aspects of the policies were then developed even further. The Conservative members of the coalition government formed in 2010 (see p 43) were also sympathetic to many of the aims of the neoliberals, and the Conservative governments after 2015 have developed neoliberal policies further, so this approach has had a lasting influence on British education.

**Examiners' notes**

Look out for 6- and 12-mark questions specifically about vocational education. You may also need to include details of policies under subsequent governments.

## New Labour

From 1997 to 2010 the Labour Party was in power, first under the leadership of Tony Blair and then, from 2007, under Gordon Brown.

Before taking power, the leadership of the Labour Party had begun describing themselves as New Labour to signal that they were no longer following traditional Labour Party policies. The New Labour philosophy was to follow a Third Way. This was neither the traditional left wing of the old Labour Party, nor the **right-wing** approach of the neoliberals, but mixed policies from both sides of the political spectrum.

## Policies influenced by social democratic philosophy

Some education policies drew on the left-wing philosophy of the social democratic approach. These aimed to produce greater equality of opportunity by providing additional help or opportunity to those from poorer backgrounds.

### Essential notes

The Third Way was partly devised by the sociologist Anthony Giddens, an adviser to Tony Blair. It claimed to follow a coherent philosophy, based on free markets, with some government intervention to make society fairer, but critics felt it lacked a clear direction.

| Details of policy | Purpose of policy |
|---|---|
| **Excellence in Cities** ||
| Extra resources provided for education in disadvantaged inner-city areas. Included learning centres with IT facilities, learning mentors, and units for children at risk of exclusion | To improve results for disadvantaged children by helping them to overcome economic and social disadvantage |
| **Sure Start** ||
| Provided extra help for pre-school children in deprived areas (e.g. play centres and home visits to advise parents on pre-school education) | To create more equal opportunity through intervening early to boost the long-term educational performance of deprived children |
| **Academies** ||
| New schools, partly sponsored by businesses, set up to replace failing comprehensive schools | To ensure that no children, particularly those in poorer areas, were educated in a very ineffective school |
| **Further education expansion and Education Maintenance Allowances** ||
| FE was expanded and participation rates increased. EMAs provided payments of up to £30 a week to children from less affluent homes continuing in education after school | To provide more opportunities in post-compulsory education for those from working-class backgrounds. EMAs were intended to reduce drop-out rates by making it more affordable to stay on in education |
| **Expansion of higher education** ||
| Number of places in higher education was increased rapidly, nearly doubling between 1990 and 2004 | To increase opportunities for people from all class backgrounds, but particularly those from the working class |

### Essential notes

Excellence in Cities and Sure Start are examples of compensatory education – additional education to help compensate the deprived for their disadvantages.

**Table 10**
New Labour education policies promoting equality

## Policies influenced by neoliberal philosophy

Other policies introduced by New Labour drew on the philosophy of the neoliberal. These were more concerned with raising standards, making education more competitive and increasing apparent choice.

### Essential notes

Value-added league tables were designed to take into account differences in student intake, but the tables with the raw exam performance figures are used more by the media and parents.

| Details of policy | Purpose of policy |
|---|---|
| **Specialist schools** ||
| Schools could specialize in one of 10 areas (e.g. computing, science, sports, humanities) and select up to 10% of pupils according to aptitude in the specialism | To increase choice as opposed to everyone going to standard comprehensive schools. Increased institutional diversity to meet the needs of individual pupils |

| Details of policy | Purpose of policy |
|---|---|
| **Use of league tables** | |
| League tables continued to be used and more details published, including 'value-added' scores based on progress | To drive up standards by fostering competition and to measure progress towards government targets. Value-added league tables intended to provide a fairer measure of schools' performance by taking some account of class differences |
| **New Deal for Young People** | |
| Provided education, training, voluntary work or subsidized jobs for unemployed young people as well as support from personal advisers | To prevent young people joining the ranks of the long-term unemployed |
| **Vocational GCSEs and A-levels** | |
| NVQs were changed into vocational GCSEs and A-levels in 2001 | To improve the status of vocational qualifications, so they were not seen as second-rate compared with academic qualifications |

**Table 11**
New Labour education policies encouraging competition and choice

### Examiners' notes

In some questions you might need to discuss the merits of league tables. Critics argue that they simply advantage the schools that are able to attract the most able and highest proportion of higher-class pupils.

## Evaluation of New Labour policies

Tomlinson (2005) criticizes these policies for

- reintroducing selection through specialist schools; this favoured the middle class who were better able to get their children into oversubscribed schools
- an over-emphasis on targets and league tables, leading to a narrow focus within education.

Although higher education was expanded, the introduction of student fees may have discouraged some people from studying for a degree.

Trowler (2003) believes New Labour underestimated the degree to which inequality in society prevents equality of opportunity in education.

McKnight et al. (2005), however, found that overall standards have risen, with improvements in GCSE, A-level and key stage tests, and a small reduction in class differences in achievement at school.

## Essential notes

Keep up-to-date on the latest policies by following the news, add key details to your notes and think about how the policies fit different perspectives on education. A useful source is the BBC website education section – www.bbc.co.uk/news/education.

## Examiners' notes

Examiners will always be impressed by knowledge of relevant contemporary events in answers to 20- and 30-mark questions.

## Examiners' notes

You can develop the discussion of privatization by using the material on globalization which is discussed in the next section.

## The coalition government 2010–15

After the general election of 2010, a coalition government was formed. This was made up mainly of Conservatives but with the support of the Liberal Democrats.

The Conservative parts of the coalition tended to favour neoliberal policies encouraging competition and choice, whereas the Liberal Democrat parts were more in favour of social democratic type policies emphasizing equality of opportunity. This led to a mixture of policies but the Conservative part of the coalition was dominant and the Minister of Education was a Conservative MP throughout.

### Conservative-influenced policies

- The coalition government encouraged all schools to become **academies** independent of local authority control. With incentives, over 60% of state schools were academies by 2015.
- Free schools were introduced. These were funded by the state but could be set up by businesses, religious organizations, parents or teachers. The idea was to give choice where existing state schools were poor. These schools could choose their own curriculum to some extent (e.g. one free school put meditation on the curriculum).
- The curriculum was made more traditional in secondary schools and a new National Curriculum was introduced that had more emphasis on traditional learning styles and traditional content (e.g. learning fractions in maths). The education minister in 2013 set out what he saw as the importance of a 'knowledge-based curriculum' emphasizing what children learned and knew rather than the acquisition of transferable skills.
- As part of these changes, A-levels were made tougher with fewer resit opportunities and vocational qualifications were downgraded in status for university entry.
- The EBacc (English Baccalaureate) was introduced, a school performance measure that only took account of pupil performance in traditional academic subjects (English, mathematics, history or geography, the sciences and a language).
- There was increasing emphasis on **privatization**, that is the involvement of private profit-making companies in the provision of education. For example, private providers now offer many services such as educational psychology previously offered by local authorities.
- Educational Maintenance Allowances (EMAs) for poorer students in sixth forms were cut.
- Some academies are privately run by academy chains.

Higher education was also affected by marketization, with student fees allowed to rise to a maximum of £9, 000 funded by loans.

### Liberal Democrat-influenced policies

Largely due to the influence of the Liberal Democrats, some policies were introduced that were aimed more at reducing inequality rather than increasing choice, encouraging privatization or producing greater competition.

These included:

- The introduction of a **pupil premium** – extra money from outside the main schools' budget (totalling £7 billion) sent direct to schools based on the number of pupils in receipt of free school meals.

- Free school meals were provided for children in reception classes and their first two years at primary school.
- Although fees were greatly increased for universities, the loans that paid for them were only repayable once graduates earned £21 000 per year or more and some students from poor backgrounds were given maintenance grants instead of loans.

## The Conservative government after 2015

In 2015 the Conservatives won an outright majority under David Cameron and were therefore able to govern without a coalition.

However, in 2016, David Cameron resigned after losing the EU referendum (Brexit vote) and was replaced by Theresa May as Conservative Prime Minister.

### Conservative policies after 2015

Policies under Cameron and May continued, but without the influence of the more left-wing Liberal Democrats.

- In 2015 David Cameron announced that every school would become an academy regardless of the wishes of parents, although in 2016 the government decided it would not be compulsory after all.
- In 2015 maintenance grants for poorer students were removed and replaced by loans.
- In 2016 it was announced that the government wanted to allow new, academically selective, grammar schools to be set up.
- The free school programme was extended.

### Evaluation of the post-2015 policies

Many of the post-2015 policies have been criticized for increasing inequality by

- cutting support for poor students
- increasing the costs of staying on in education
- making it possible for elitist free schools and academies to develop within the state education system.

The **attainment gap** (the percentage difference between poor pupils in receipt of free school meals and other pupils getting five or more good GCSEs) rose slightly between 2010–11 and 2013–14.

Even the pupil premium was criticized (Ratcliffe, 2014) because much of the money was not spent on poorer children but was used to plug a funding gap in other areas of schools' budgets.

Critics, therefore, believed that educational policies were primarily going to benefit middle- and upper-class pupils and students and provide opportunities for private companies to profit from state education.

The diversification of schooling was also criticized for being divisive, for example by allowing new free schools based upon religious beliefs. Three state schools in Birmingham were criticized by OFSTED, for example, for allegedly being Islamized and potentially encouraging radicalization of the pupils (the so-called Trojan Horse affair).

## Conclusion

Recent policies have been characterized by what Stephen Ball (2011) calls **fragmented centralization** with comprehensive secondary education being replaced by a wide variety of competing schools but central government dictating to schools in some respects (e.g. by forcing them to become academies).

**Examiners' notes**

Remember to discuss even more recent policies. Keep up-to-date with the news and add to your notes on education as new policies are introduced.

**Essential notes**

Whether increased universities fees discouraged poor students from taking up university places is disputed but there is strong evidence that this encouraged them to study closer to home and to continue to live with parents, sometimes at the expense of going to a prestigious university.

**Examiners' notes**

The material on post-2015 policies is very useful for answering questions on class differences in attainment as well as questions on educational policy.

## Globalization and education

**Globalization** is the process by which different parts of the world become less isolated and more interconnected so that individual countries are less self-contained.

### Globalization

Roland Robertson defines globalization as referring to 'both the compression of the world and the intensification of consciousness the world as a whole' (1992, p 8).

Physical difference between different parts of the world becomes less important, people become more aware of parts of the world outside their locality and of the world as a whole, and national boundaries become less significant.

In the UK, globalization has a range of impacts and it involves processes such as:

- transnational companies operating in the British economy
- large-scale international trade
- large-scale tourism
- high levels of migration
- ideas, popular culture and academic knowledge from abroad influencing the UK
- transnational political organizations such as the United Nations and the World Trade Organization influencing the UK.

### Globalization and schools

Education appears to be largely controlled and influenced by national governments and to be relatively unaffected by globalization.

However, Anthony Kelly (2009) discusses competing theories of the effects of globalization on educational policy.

- Educational policies may be increasingly designed to produce workers who can compete in the global economy and therefore economic factors influence educational policies more and more.
- This results in reduced emphasis upon social policies such as creating equality of opportunity or encouraging social integration.
- Education systems throughout the world may become more similar as they try to achieve the same objectives with an increasing worldwide trend towards marketization.
- As multinational corporations become more involved in education, similar school improvement programmes might be introduced in different parts of the world.
- The professional independence of autonomy of teachers might be undermined as managers and consultants play an increasing role in education.

Some of these trends are demonstrated by the involvement of companies such as Pearson in British, American and other education systems.

Private schools also come to rely increasingly on overseas students and some are setting up overseas schools.

### Examiners' notes

You may get AS or A-level questions about globalization and education of any length. For 20- and 30-mark questions you should include a definition of globalization and a brief explanation of what it is.

### Examiners' notes

Even if you don't get a specific question about globalization, it can be very useful to discuss it to get in to higher mark bands in questions about other topics. For example, you could include it to question the functionalist view that education helps to integrate populations within society or to support Marxist views about the influence of business on education.

## Globalization in higher education

Educational institutions that operate globally increasingly need to be run as businesses because they are unlikely to be able to rely on government support if their activities cross national boundaries.

Stephen Ball (2012) points out that universities have become increasingly global institutions, opening up their products to global audiences.

They have done this by

- setting up subsidiaries in other countries (e.g. Lancaster University has a joint venture in China)
- offering online courses to a global audience
- trying to attract overseas students (who can be charged higher levels of fees than domestic students).

Many universities also employ staff from a wide variety of countries. The globalization of universities can be seen as helping to subsidize provision for domestic students or as denying places to domestic students depending upon your viewpoint.

### Multinational companies and education

Stephen Ball (2012) and others see a close link between globalization, neoliberalism and the increasing involvement of private companies in education. Many of these companies are multinational and operate across national boundaries.

To Ball, this reduces the control of national governments over education and tends to produce a further move towards neoliberal policies.

However, globalization could have other effects in education. For example, increased migration could lead to a more **multicultural curriculum** and greater understanding of different cultures within educational institutions.

## Conclusion

Education continues to be predominantly a concern of individual nations but national policies can be influenced by globalization as governments seek to compete in the world economy and they sometimes copy policies from other countries.

Multinational corporations can play a direct role in spreading educational policies across the globe.

However, the influence of globalization shouldn't be exaggerated. State primary and secondary education are still being largely shaped by national governments.

**Examiners' notes**

This material is useful for discussing neoliberal perspectives on education and may help you get into top mark bands for questions both on theories of education and on educational policy.

## The purpose of research

Social research can be conducted for a number of purposes.

- It can be used to test existing theories. Researchers conduct **experiments** to test a particular **hypothesis** (a prediction about what is likely to happen). They decide whether the hypothesis is supported or contradicted, based on their observations of the results of these experiments.
- It can be used to develop new theories. By observing social life, the researcher can produce new ideas about how some aspects of society works or what causes particular types of social behaviour.

**Methodology** is concerned with the methods used to collect data and the philosophy underlying the production of sociological data.

## Types of data

Research can involve producing or using different types of data.

1. **Quantitative data** consists of data in a numerical form; for example, statistics about the number of girls and boys passing an exam.
2. **Qualitative data** is any data that is not numerical; for example, written descriptions, diaries, photographs, recorded music or radio programmes.

Data sources can be divided into two types.

1. **Primary sources** are those sources of data that are produced directly by the sociologist conducting research; for example, resulting from a **questionnaire** or interview.
2. **Secondary sources** consist of existing data produced by someone else but used by the sociologist.

### Examiners' notes

This section introduces the basic terms you may be asked to explain for a 4-mark AS question. They also provide a foundation for all longer questions about methodology on AS and A-level papers. You need to be able to define the terms highlighted in bold.

| Type of data | Primary source | Secondary source |
|---|---|---|
| **Quantitative** | Numerical data from research conducted by a sociologist (e.g. statistics from a questionnaire) | Existing numerical data (e.g. official government statistics) |
| **Qualitative** | Non-numerical data from a sociological study (e.g. notes on the observation of a classroom) | Non-numerical data from existing material (e.g. content of diaries or email messages) |

**Table 12**
Types of data

Many individual studies use a mixture of qualitative and qualitative data and primary and secondary sources.

## Evaluating data

No data produced by research is perfect, as all types of data have limitations. These can be considered in terms of the following concepts:

1. **Reliability**. Data is reliable if another researcher using identical methods would produce the same results. Reliable data can be checked through the research being reproduced or **replicated**;

for example, reviewing registration details of the number of people attending an event or sitting an exam. Unreliable data is data that would not be confirmed by a repeat of the same study.

2. **Validity** concerns how true data is, that is, how close the fit is between the data and reality. Data is invalid if it does not match reality. For example, invalid data might be produced if respondents to interviews do not tell the truth.

3. **Representativeness** and **generalizability**. Data is representative if the individuals or examples studied are a typical cross-section of the wider population or group that the researcher is interested in. If the individuals or examples are representative, then it is legitimate to make generalizations about the wider group they represent.

## Choosing research topics

A sociologist's choice of topic to investigate is influenced by the following factors:

1. **Practical issues**
   Researchers need to choose topics for which it is feasible to develop and conduct valid research. For example, if a specific group needs to be studied in relation to a particular topic, it must be possible to identify and then get access to members of this group. Another practical consideration relates to the availability of research grants. Most researchers rely upon funding, which may come directly from research councils that distribute money from the government, charities or businesses. The choice of research topic tends to reflect the availability of funds.

2. **Ethical issues**
   Ethics concern whether research is seen as morally acceptable. Research may be seen as unethical if
   - it harms the subjects of the research
   - the subjects are unable or unwilling to give **informed consent** (they must be aware of the research, understand it and be in a position to agree to take part)
   - it is impossible to maintain **confidentiality** by keeping the identity of the subjects secret
   - the research could be used to help individuals or organizations carry out illegal or immoral acts.

3. **Theoretical issues**
   Researchers are inevitably influenced by their own values about what they believe to be important. For example, feminist researchers are more likely to choose topics concerned with gender inequality than other types of researchers.
   The importance of a topic might relate to how it is linked to the introduction of new social policies, to understanding developments in society, or because it can be used to examine influential theories within sociology.

**Essential notes**

Sociological data may be reliable but invalid. For example, if data from questionnaires is accurately compiled and would be confirmed in a repeat of the questionnaire, but the respondents have not responded truthfully.

**Examiners' notes**

Evaluating research methods is usually the main focus of the 16-mark AS 'Methods' question on Paper 2 and may be crucial to the 10-mark 'Outline and explain' A-level questions as well. It provides the foundation for the 20-mark 'Methods in context' question too, and may be of relevance to the 20-mark 'Theory and methods' question on A-level Paper 3, so understanding these concepts and being able to apply them is essential.

**Essential notes**

Theoretical issues such as the preferred perspective or approach of the sociologist might seem the most important, but in reality, practicality trumps theoretical and ethical issues; if it is impractical to carry out some research then it is unlikely to be attempted.

☞ **This topic continues on the next two pages**

## Research methods and sources

Sociologists use a number of different research methods or sources.

- **Experiment**: Researchers set up an artificial situation and manipulate it to test their theory. Rosenthal and Jacobson (1968) tested the theory of the self-fulfilling prophecy by giving teachers false information about the IQ scores of pupils (see p 34).
- **Questionnaire**: A written list of questions that are answered by respondents. J.W.B. Douglas (1970) used questionnaires alongside other methods to study the factors influencing attainment in different social classes.
- **Interview**: Verbal questioning of one or more people by a researcher. William Labov (1973) used interviews to study the linguistic ability of children.
- **Observation/participant observation**: Researcher watches an event or behaviour and records the observations. In participant observation, the researcher takes part in the events being observed. Cecile Wright (1992) conducted classroom observation to study racism in education.
- **Official statistics**: Numerical data produced by government agencies. McKnight et al. (2005) used data from official statistics on qualifications to evaluate the effectiveness of the Labour government's policies.
- **Documents**: Any physical artefact containing information that could be used by a sociologist. Leon Feinstein (2003) used data from the National Child Development Study to examine factors shaping educational achievement.

## Selecting research methods

Various factors influence the choice of research method; these are generally similar to the issues which affect the choice of topic.

1. **Practical** issues – for example, ease of access to the group, availability of funding and time constraints.
2. **Ethical** issues – for example, participant safety, informed consent and confidentiality.
3. **Theoretical** issues – whether the data produced will be valid and reliable.

## Philosophies of research

Two broad theoretical approaches to research methods can be identified.

### Positivism

Positivism is an early influential approach, advocated by Auguste Comte (1840s) and Émile Durkheim (1897), which suggests that sociology can be scientific. Positivists believe:

- There are **objective social facts** about the social world. These facts can be expressed in statistics.
- You can look for **correlations** – patterns in which two or more things tend to occur together.

- Correlations may represent **causal relationships** (one thing causing another).
- It is possible to discover **laws** of human behaviour – causes of behaviour that are true for all humans throughout history.
- Human behaviour is shaped by external stimuli (things that happen to us) rather than internal stimuli (what goes on in the mind).
- To be scientific you should only study what you can observe; that is, not emotions, meanings or motives, which cannot be observed.
- This perspective supports the use of quantitative methods such as official statistics, which provide factual data.

## The interpretive approach

**Interpretivists** usually advocate the use of qualitative data to interpret social action, with an emphasis on the meanings and motives of participants. From this viewpoint

- people do not simply react to external stimuli, but interpret the **meaning** of stimuli before reacting
- an understanding of people's unobservable subjective states is required. This cannot be reduced to statistical data.

Methods therefore have to be used which reveal these meanings, motives, emotions and beliefs. These include in-depth interviews and participant observation.

Not all sociologists support an exclusively interpretive or positivist approach; many use elements from both approaches. For example, they may collect statistics but also use qualitative data to understand the reasons for the behaviour that produces the statistics.

**Examiners' notes**

Contrast these approaches to develop more in-depth analysis. Explain why positivists tend to criticize qualitative and subjective methods and interpretivists tend to criticize more quantitative and 'scientific' methods if you are asked to evaluate particular methods in extended questions.

### The purpose of sampling

Instead of studying an entire **population** (the group of interest in a particular study) the researcher usually selects a small sample that is representative of the population as a whole. The sociologist can then generalize about the larger population on the basis of the group studied.

- The **sampling unit** is the individual thing or person in that population.
- The **sampling frame** is a list of all those in the population (for example, the Electoral Roll is a sampling frame of those eligible to vote).

**Examiners' notes**

The terms defined above are typical concepts to be outlined in 4-mark questions.

### Types of sampling

There are a variety of ways of producing a sample. **Table 13** summarizes the advantages and disadvantages of each.

**Table 13**
Types of sampling

| Type of sampling | How it is conducted | Advantages/ why it is used | Disadvantages |
|---|---|---|---|
| Random | Every sampling unit has an equal chance of being chosen (e.g. drawn out of a hat) | Technically, the most representative, as it relies upon statistical odds | Large sample needed to ensure that statistically it is likely to be representative |
| Stratified random | Population divided into groups according to important **variables** (e.g. class, gender, ethnicity). Sample then chosen in same proportions as found in population | Relatively small sample can be used with confidence that it is still representative | Requires sampling frame which includes details of significant characteristics of population being studied |
| Quota | Establishes predetermined number of people with each particular characteristic. Once quota is filled no more people in that category are included | Advantages of stratified random sampling but can be conducted without variables being available from sampling frame | Accessibility of potential respondents affects their chances of being included in the sample. May be less representative than random and stratified random sampling |
| Multi-stage | Involves taking a sample of a sample (e.g. a sample of voters in a sample of constituencies) | Allows a broad-based sample while saving time and money through not including all the potential sources | Less truly representative than some methods, as many members of the population have no chance of being selected |

| Type of sampling | How it is conducted | Advantages/ Why it is used | Disadvantages |
|---|---|---|---|
| Snowballing | Members of a sample put researcher in touch with other potential members | Used mainly with groups who are hard to identify or access (e.g. criminals) | Very unlikely to be truly representative, since based on people who have contact with one another |
| Opportunity | People chosen on basis of being easily accessible and willing to participate in research | Tends to be easiest, cheapest and quickest way of collecting a sample and may lead to a good **response rate** | Makes no attempt to be truly representative, so cannot generalize from the findings |

**Examiners' notes**

Be prepared to identify two advantages or two problems with any of these sampling methods and to explain them for 10-mark A-level questions. For 16-mark AS questions you can gain evaluation points for noting the limitations of the sampling in a study, particularly in essay questions about social surveys and questionnaires.

## Non-representative sampling

Members of a sample may be picked for being untypical of a population or to study specific characteristics. This **non-representative sampling** is used

- to **falsify** (prove wrong) a general theory by looking for exceptions to a pattern. Margaret Fuller (1984) studied a sample of African-Caribbean girls who were very successful in the education system even though overall rates of success for this ethnic group were relatively low.
- to find the **key informants** who can provide information about an area of social life because they have special insights or expertise (for example, criminals).

## Case studies

Another highly unrepresentative form of sampling is to use a particular **case study**. Case studies can be used:

- to develop a comprehensive understanding of something by studying it in depth
- to develop a general theoretical approach by falsifying a theory or proving it wrong
- to develop **typologies** (for example, different school subcultures)
- to generate new hypotheses or theories.

A problem with case studies is that you cannot generalize from them. Bryman (1988) suggests that this can be overcome through using multiple case studies. However, it can be difficult to compare the findings of case studies carried out by different researchers.

## Life histories

A **life history** is a case study of one person's life. An example is Thomas and Znaniecki's (1919) study of Jenny, an ageing woman. Plummer (1982) suggests that these are useful for helping understand the world from an individual's point of view. However, they are highly unrepresentative and cannot be used to make generalizations.

**Examiners' notes**

You are most likely to get short questions about non-representative sampling, case studies or life histories, but it is unlikely you will get a long question on these topics.

## Social surveys

**Social surveys** are large-scale studies, which collect standardized data about large groups, often using questionnaires.

- **Factual surveys** collect descriptive information.
- **Attitudes surveys** examine subjective opinions (for example, opinion polls).
- **Explanatory surveys** test theories or produce hypotheses.

## Pilot studies

A **pilot study** is a small-scale trial study conducted before the main study in order to test the feasibility of the main study and to refine the research methods being used.

They can be used to

- test how useful and unambiguous interview questions are
- develop ways to gain the cooperation of respondents
- develop the research skills of the researchers
- decide whether or not to proceed with research.

## Conducting questionnaires

Questionnaires consist of a written list of questions. When planning this type of research the researcher has to choose how to administer the questionnaire. A key consideration will be what level of response rate is required; that is, what proportion of questionnaires need to be completed and returned. **Table 14** summarizes the options and the main advantages and disadvantages of their different approaches.

| Method of administering questionnaire | Main advantages | Main disadvantages |
|---|---|---|
| Face-to-face | Relatively high response rate<br><br>Interviewer can clarify questions | Interviewer may influence responses (**interviewer bias**)<br><br>Time-consuming for both subject and interviewer, therefore potentially expensive |
| Telephone | Relatively cheap, and easy to access a geographically dispersed **sample** | Response rates may be low, limited to subjects who are prepared to take part in telephone research<br><br>Respondents may be influenced by voice of interviewer |

**Examiners' notes**

A typical 4-mark question might be to outline two reasons why people contuct pilot studies.

**Examiners' notes**

16-mark AS essay questions about questionnaires or surveys are likely to specify a particular type. Make sure you write about the specific issues related to administering this type as well as general advantages and disadvantages.

| Method of administering questionnaire | Main advantages | Main disadvantages |
|---|---|---|
| Postal | Relatively cheap and easy to access a geographically dispersed sample<br><br>No interviewer bias from direct contact | Response rates tend to be very low<br><br>Respondents may not be typical of the population as a whole |
| Internet | Very cheap and quick to send to a widely dispersed sample | Response rate is likely to be low<br><br>Limited to those with internet access and not inclined to delete spam |

**Table 14**
Ways of administering questionnaires

Researchers also have to develop the questions to collect reliable data on what are often abstract concepts or theories. This is called **operationalizing** concepts (see p 57). Deciding what types of questions to include and how to word them is a real skill. **Table 15** summarizes the advantages and disadvantages of different types of questions.

| Type of question | Description | Advantages | Disadvantages |
|---|---|---|---|
| **Fixed-choice** | Respondents are given a restricted range of options to choose from (e.g. agree/disagree, yes/no) or asked to use a ratings scale (e.g. from 1 to 10) | Easy to produce statistical data and to analyse answers<br><br>Good for testing existing theories and producing **reliable** data which can be checked<br><br>Positivists see answers as social facts | No opportunity for respondents to clarify concepts or qualify views<br><br>Generally poor for collecting information about feelings, meanings or motives<br><br>Not favoured by interpretivists |
| **Open-ended** | Respondents are asked the question and can provide their own unprompted response | Can produce more in-depth data and better for discovering complex feelings, meanings or motives<br><br>Preferred by interpretivists | Answers need to be interpreted to produce quantitative data<br><br>Difficult and time-consuming to produce statistical data<br><br>Less favoured by positivists |

## Essential notes

Questions can also administered using the internet. For example, Cleland (2016) used message boards on football sites to collect data on fans' views on racism. This allowed him to collect qualitative data on immediate reactions to events, but the self-selection of respondents made the representativeness of the sample questionable. The method also raised ethical issues about informed consent, privacy of participants and identity deception by participants.

## Essential notes

The Likert scale in fixed-choice questions measures respondents who are asked to say whether they strongly agree or agree, or strongly disagree or disagree with a statement.

**Table 15**
Advantages and disadvantages of fixed-choice and open-ended questions

☞ This topic continues on the next two pages

### The advantages of questionnaires

- large amounts of data can be collected quickly
- little personal involvement by researchers
- access to subjects is easy
- no great ethical issues since research cannot be conducted secretly and filling in the questionnaire implies consent
- easy to quantify the results, find correlations and use statistical analysis to look for causes
- everyone responds to the same stimuli so positivists see differences in answers as reflecting real differences
- comparative analysis and replication (repeating the questionnaire) are easy, making the results reliable
- a large, geographically dispersed sample can be used, increasing the representativeness of the data and the ability to generalize.

For positivists, the statistical patterns revealed can be used to develop new theories; and questionnaires can be devised to test existing theories.

Non-positivists see questionnaires as useful for collecting straightforward, descriptive data.

### The disadvantages of questionnaires

Interpretive sociologists question the use of questionnaires for a range of reasons.

- When designing questionnaires, researchers assume that they know what is important, so find it difficult to develop novel hypotheses.
- The operationalization of concepts distorts the social world by shaping concepts that are in line with researchers' rather than respondents' meanings.
- Different answers may not reflect real differences between respondents, as they may have interpreted the questions differently.
- The validity of the data may be undermined by deliberate lying, faulty memory or respondents not fully understanding their own motivations. People may not act in line with questionnaire answers. For example, people may deny being racist even though they act in racist ways.
- The coding of open-ended data distorts the distinct answers given by individuals.
- There could be an ethical issue of confidentiality unless the questionnaires are handled carefully.
- Researchers are distant from their subjects, making it difficult to understand the social world from their viewpoint. Interaction cannot be understood through questionnaires.
- To feminist researchers, questionnaires preclude the possibility of subjects evaluating the research.

Most sociologists accept that surveys are useful for collecting factual or descriptive data, but there is controversy over their use in explanatory studies.

### Examiners' notes

Discussing the advantages and disadvantages of questionnaire research is a typical 16-mark AS question and may feature in a 10-mark A-level 'Outline and explain' question as well. It can be useful to break your answer down into practical, ethical and theoretical issues. Then try to include why positivists would support this type of research and interpretivists would criticize it. Use examples to get higher marks. 10-mark A-level questions asking you to 'outline and explain' two advantages and disadvantages do not need so much structure, but depth on theoretical issues is useful, as are examples.

## Operationalizing concepts

Researchers also have to develop the questions to collect valid and reliable data on what are often abstract concepts or theories. This process is called operationalizing concepts.

Operationalizing involves putting a concept in a form that allows it to be measured. This process is crucial to ensure that the concept is accurately measured (valid) and that each time they are used, every respondent understands the concept in the same way (reliable). Usually this is achieved by identifying indicators for the concept – easily measurable categories that, when put together, give a clear picture of whether or not the concept applies.

For example, asking respondents how religious they are would produce a range of answers that could not be easily compared, because respondents would understand the term 'religious' in different ways. However, the concept of 'religious' could be operationalized by identifying several indicators of being religious. These might include whether and how often the respondent attends religious services or prays, whether they believe in God(s) and religious texts, whether religious teachings affect their lifestyle and so on. The answers to these questions would need to be in a form that could be compared, so the respondent is usually given a number of fixed alternatives from which to select. This type of question is known as a closed or fixed-choice question – rather than freedom to write or say whatever they like – an open or open-ended question (see p 55).

## Structured and unstructured interviews

Interviews can be defined, simply, as one or more researchers asking questions to one or more respondents. They can have various degrees of structure depending on the extent to which the questions are pre-determined.

| Degree of structure | Advantages | Disadvantages |
|---|---|---|
| **Structured** – pre-set questions asked in same order without variation | Favoured by quantitative researchers<br><br>Easier to replicate and compare results<br><br>Less chance of interviewer bias | No opportunity for probing deeper<br><br>Less chance of discovering new hypotheses<br><br>Harder to discover what is important to the respondents |
| **Semi-structured** – some fixed questions with list of topics to be covered | Provide some opportunity for respondents to lead the interviews while ensuring main topics are covered | Lacks specific advantages of both structured and unstructured interviews |
| **Unstructured** – few or no fixed questions, more like a conversation | Favoured by qualitative researchers<br><br>Allow respondents to direct the interview<br><br>More opportunity for developing new hypotheses | Hard to replicate<br><br>Time-consuming<br><br>Difficult to compare interviews<br><br>May go off-track |

**Table 16**
Degrees of structure in interviews

## Interviewing styles

Most interviewers use a **non-directive** form of interviewing. In this case the interviewer offers no opinions of their own and does not express approval or disapproval of the responses. Most sociologists regard this as being the most objective way to interview people.

Howard Becker (1970) advocated a more aggressive style of interviewing in which the statements of the interviewees are challenged. Which interviewing Chicago school teachers he used this style to uncover some racist feelings among the teachers, which he believed they would otherwise have kept hidden.

Feminist interviewers such as Ann Oakley (1981) advocate **collaborative interviewing**. Here the researcher befriends the interviewee. Valid data emerges from the development of a relationship between the interviewer and the interviewee. Oakley sees this as the most valid and ethical type of interviewing, since she thinks more truthful data will result.

| Type of interview | Advantages | Disadvantages |
|---|---|---|
| Individual | Prevents respondents from being influenced by others<br><br>Less time-consuming | No opportunity to observe interaction |
| Group | Can observe interaction<br><br>Encourages deeper thought about issues and more developed answers<br><br>Closer to normal social life | Respondents may be influenced by desire to conform to views of others<br><br>Dominant members of a group can sway opinion of others |

**Table 17**
Individual and **group interviews**

**Examiners' notes**

Mentioning feminism can add some theoretical depth to help you reach the top mark band for 16-mark questions or in any A-level 10-mark questions.

## The main advantages of interviews

Both positivists and interpretivists find interviews useful. The main advantages are practicality and flexibility. **Tables 16** and **17** outline the specific advantages associated with particular types of interviews.

- Quantitative researchers prefer interviews to participant observation – larger samples can be used, statistical data can be produced with the coding of answers, and the research can be replicated to increase reliability.
- Qualitative researchers prefer interviews to questionnaires because concepts can be clarified and there is more opportunity for respondents to express ideas in their own way, say what is important to them and explore issues in depth.
- To feminists, interviews have theoretical advantages, since they provide space for critical reflection, collaboration and interaction between interviewer and interviewee.

**Essential notes**

Remember to use as many technical terms as possible in answers to Research Methods questions.

## The main disadvantages of interviews

- As with questionnaires, the validity of interview data may be affected by respondents being untruthful.
- Answers can be affected by faulty memory or people not fully understanding their own behaviour.
- Interviewers might lead respondents towards preferred answers.
- The presence of the researcher might influence answers.
- Social factors such as ethnicity may influence the sort of answers members of different social groups are willing to give.

**Examiners' notes**

You can develop essays on the advantages and disadvantages of interviews with reference to examples from education (or elsewhere) and by explaining the somewhat mixed opinions of positivists and interpretivists.

## Conclusion

The practicality and flexibility of interviews make them attractive to researchers and they are widely used. Hammersley and Gomm (2004) believe that interview data remains useful when combined with other methods but should be handled carefully.

## Observation

Observation simply involves looking at something and recording data.

Positivists see observation as essential; for example, when observing the results of experiments.

Interpretive sociologists are much more likely to use participant observation than positivists. They tend to use observation in the context of studying normal social life. The study of a way of life of a social group is known as ethnography.

Observation of social groups can be subjective, since the observer has to choose what exactly to take note of. However, some observers use more systematic methods to produce quantitative data. For example, Flander's Interaction Analysis Categories (FIAC) (1970) categorizes classroom interaction into 10 categories so that researchers can quantify what takes place.

## Participant observation – overt and covert research

Participant observation involves the researcher joining in with the group being studied. The level to which they participate can vary.

They can be a full participant observer, or a partial participant observer.

### A full participant observer
- may develop a deeper understanding through sharing experiences
- is likely to see a full range of behaviours
- may influence the group less than an outside observer
- may find him- or herself taking part in illegal or immoral activities
- may lose objectivity and 'go native'
- may influence the group through joining in activities.

### A partial participant observer
- can easily observe groups who are different to the observer
- can commit less time to observation
- can avoid involvement in illegal or immoral activities
- may find that subjects act less naturally
- will not share the full range of group experiences.

The researcher also has to decide whether to be open (overt) or secretive (covert).

### Overt participation
- allows the observer to ask questions
- allows the observer to retain some detachment
- removes the need to lie and risk being 'uncovered'
- risks influencing the behaviour of the subjects
- makes it difficult to become a full participant
- may encounter resistance from groups not wishing to be observed.

### Covert participation
- enables respondents to act more naturally
- makes it difficult to access some groups
- can be considered unethical, as it misleads subjects
- makes it difficult to opt out of illegal or immoral activities

- can render the observer liable to lose objectivity by becoming one of the group.

## The advantages of participant observation

Many sociologists regard participant observation as having a high degree of validity.

Interpretivists, in particular, support participant observation because it allows an understanding of the subjective viewpoints of individuals and the processes of interaction in which people's meanings, motives and self-concepts constantly change. It therefore avoids a static picture of social life. Other advantages include the following:

- It can sometimes be done with little preparation and conducted by a single researcher, making the initial costs quite small.
- Researchers are less likely than in other methods to impose their own concepts, structures and preconceptions on the data.
- It may gain answers to questions that had not been anticipated and were not included in questionnaires or interviews.
- It is difficult for respondents to lie or mislead.
- The researcher understands subjects better because she or he experiences some of the same things.
- It provides in-depth studies that can be useful both for developing new theories and for falsifying existing ones.

## The limitations and disadvantages of participant observation

To positivists, participant observation is an unsystematic, subjective and unscientific method. Even for interpretivists, there are several problems:

- It can be time-consuming for the researcher and may end up being costly as the researcher has to support her- or himself.
- The researchers' lives may be disrupted; they may need to do illegal/immoral things or they may face dangers.
- There can be practical difficulties about recording the data, especially in covert research when notes cannot be taken at the time.
- The researcher is limited to studying a small number of people in a single place.
- The samples are likely to be too small for generalizations.
- It will be impossible to join some groups to carry out observation.
- The studies cannot be replicated, so the results may be unreliable, and comparisons difficult.
- Interpretations are rather subjective as the researcher has to be very selective about what is reported.
- The presence of the researcher will change group behaviour and affect the validity of the data.
- Covert participant observation can be regarded as unethical because it involves lying to those being studied.

### Examiners' notes

When answering a 16-mark AS question, explain why interpretivists see this as more valid than other methods because it is closer to real social life, while positivists see it as too subjective, unreliable and unscientific to be of much use. Developing these sorts of points is likely to impress the examiner, and they are also useful in 10-mark A-level questions.

## Conclusion

Participant observation is advocated by interpretivists as being the only research method that gets close to real social life and is therefore the most valid research method. It is criticized by positivists for being highly subjective, impossible to replicate, and therefore unreliable.

## Longitudinal studies

Longitudinal studies involve the study of a group of people over an extended period of time. They are sometimes also known as **panel studies**. Often data is collected periodically, with the respondents being asked to provide information perhaps every few months or every few years.

Longitudinal research can use a wide range of methods; for example, periodic **focus groups** or group interviews. However, the most common method is the use of questionnaires. Longitudinal research may also make some use of secondary sources. An important longitudinal study into the causes of educational underachievement by the working class was conducted by J.W.B Douglas (1970).

## The advantages of longitudinal research

This type of research has several advantages:

- It allows the researcher to look at processes over time.
- It does not require respondents to recall information retrospectively, therefore the data may be more valid than conventional research.
- It is invaluable for studying topics that look at long-term changes over an individual's **life course**; for example, looking at **social mobility**, factors influencing long-term health or the relationship between educational achievement and occupational status.

## Problems with longitudinal research

There are a number of problems with conducting longitudinal research:

- It requires a very long-term commitment from researchers.
- Because of the extended time-period, it tends to be extremely expensive.
- Once the research has been started, it is not possible to collect retrospective information, so a wide range of data is usually collected in the beginning, before it becomes clear what the most relevant data is going be, thus adding to the expense.
- The sample size is likely to get smaller as people drop out or disappear. Those remaining may be untypical of the sample as a whole, making it difficult to compare results over time.
- The sample may become less representative over time if the population it is designed to represent changes some of its characteristics.
- The fact that people are taking part in a research project might make them think more about their behaviour and therefore influence the outcomes of the research, making it less valid.

## Triangulation

**Triangulation** involves the use of three or more sources of data or research methods in the course of a single study. A researcher might use more than one primary source, and also use secondary data. Although positivists advocate the use of exclusively quantitative sources, and interpretivists prefer qualitative sources, in practice many studies combine both types of source.

**Examiners' notes**

There are not many examples of this type of study, because they are so time-consuming and expensive, so it is worth learning about a couple of examples from educational research.

**Examiners' notes**

This is probably most likely to crop up as a short question (possibly 10 marks), but make sure you are familiar with all these advantages and disadvantages in case you get an essay question.

**Examiners' notes**

Triangulation is useful for concluding discussions about any single method. Point out that each method can be complemented with other methods that provide different types of data or help to fill in the gaps.

## Types of triangulation

Hammersley (1996) distinguishes three ways of combining methods:

1. Triangulation – findings are cross-checked using a variety of methods. For example, interviews are used to check the responses made in questionnaires.
2. **Facilitation** – one method is used to assist or develop the use of another method. For example, when in-depth interviews are used to devise questionnaire questions.
3. **Complementarity** – different methods are combined to dovetail different aspects of an investigation. For example, questionnaires are used to discover overall statistical patterns and participant observation is used to reveal the reasons for those patterns.

## The purposes of triangulation

Bryman (2001) identifies 10 uses of triangulation.

1. To check the reliability of data produced using different methods.
2. Qualitative research facilitating quantitative research; for example, by designing questionnaire questions.
3. Quantitative research facilitating qualitative research; for example, by helping to identify people for a sample.
4. Filling in the gaps where the main research method cannot produce all the necessary data.
5. Using some methods to study static features of social life and others to study changes.
6. Using different methods to obtain different perspectives from research subjects.
7. Using different methods to help to generalize.
8. Using qualitative research to understand the relationship between variables revealed in the quantitative research.
9. Studying different aspects of a phenomenon.
10. Solving an unexplained result by using a different method to that initially used.

Bryman sees multi-strategy research as very useful, as the limitations and disadvantages of each individual research method can be partially overcome.

## An example of triangulation

Cecile Wright (1992) used the following four combination of methods to investigate racism in primary schools:

1. Classroom observation to see how teachers actually behaved.
2. Examination of documents about test results to examine the effects of racism.
3. Interviews with headteachers to investigate school policies.
4. Informal interviews with teachers to uncover unobservable attitudes.

### Essential notes

Triangulation is becoming increasingly common in sociology as it becomes more and more accepted that neither quantitative nor qualitative data can provide a full picture. Positivist and interpretivist approaches tend to lend themselves to different research questions and different topics, so they can often complement each other rather than being mutually exclusive.

### Examiners' notes

You can argue that each research method is useful for certain types of study but research is usually strengthened by the use of more than one method.

### Examiners' notes

This study uses several methods, so it can be used to illustrate a range of individual methods as applied to education.

## Types of secondary sources and documents

Secondary sources are data that already exist. Secondary source documents can be any physical artefact that contains meaningful material produced by people. This includes images, sounds and digital data, as well as printed documents with words and statistics.

- Documents may be produced by agencies such as the government, research bodies or companies (**public documents**), or individuals (**personal documents**).
- They can be quantitative (for example, government statistics) or qualitative (for example, letters and diaries).
- They can be historical or contemporary.

## The uses of secondary sources

Secondary sources are usually used for practical reasons.

- They save time and money, since they already exist and therefore do not require expensive primary research.
- Many secondary sources include data that are beyond the scope of sociologists to collect (for example, **census** data).
- They allow the study of societies in the past for which it is impossible to produce primary sources.
- They allow insights into aspects of social life that may not be accessible to researchers (for example, intimate family life).

A major disadvantage of secondary sources is that they are produced by non-sociologists for their own purposes. Therefore they may not include the specific data that sociologists are interested in, or the data may be collected without the rigour that sociologists use.

- They may use categories or concepts that do not fit with sociological theories.
- The categories used may change, making comparisons over time difficult. For example, the government has changed definitions of poverty and unemployment.

## Government statistics

Government statistics cover a wide range of topics including demography, crime, unemployment, educational achievement and participation, births, deaths, marriages and divorce. The government also conducts statistical surveys such as the General Household Survey. Since 1801 it has carried out a census every decade, in which participation is compulsory.

## Positivist views of official statistics

Positivists generally view official statistics as both valid and reliable. Durkheim (1970), for example, used suicide statistics, which he regarded as social facts, to investigate the causes of suicide.

Some sociologists admit that government statistics may be unreliable, but believe it is still possible to use them to produce reliable and valid data. For example, they believe that reliable crime statistics can be produced if surveys are conducted to supplement the information collected by the police.

| Type of government crime statistics | How they are collected | Why they are useful | Main problems |
|---|---|---|---|
| Statistics on crimes known to the police | Police stations record events they believe to be criminal | Provides an estimate of the total number of crimes committed | Many crimes are not reported to the police<br><br>Police have discretion in deciding which events to record |
| The British Crime Survey | Annual social survey using questionnaires to ask a sample of householders if they have been victims of crime | Provides an estimate of unreported crime | Respondents may not be truthful<br><br>Interpretation is still required as to whether crime has taken place<br><br>Sample may not be truly representative<br><br>Not all crimes are included |

**Table 18**
Government crime statistics

## Interpretivist views of official statistics

From the interpretivist point of view, official statistics are not facts but merely an interpretation produced by government agencies. They argue that it is impossible to produce objective, reliable and valid statistics.

Interpretivists point out that all data requires classification and interpretation. For example, in crime statistics, the police, the Crown Prosecution Service and courts all have considerable discretion in determining whether a crime has taken place and whether a particular individual has committed the crime. To Cicourel (1976), the subjective classifications of police and courts makes this data invalid.

In another example, Maxwell Atkinson (1978) saw suicide statistics as the product of police and coroners' taken-for-granted assumptions about the sort of people who commit suicide.

## Conclusion

- Some statistics may be relatively reliable and valid. For example, death statistics are highly reliable since the vast majority of deaths are likely to be recorded, and they are valid since it is easy to classify whether someone is alive or not.
- Some statistics are much less reliable and valid, such as crime statistics, because there is a large 'dark figure' of unrecorded crime and there is often considerable room for personal opinion in determining whether crime has taken place.
- Official statistics are nevertheless very useful, even if they are imperfect, because they are often the best available data on a topic.

### Examiners' notes

In essay questions about official statistics, examine both viewpoints. This will allow you to score high marks for analysis and to introduce the evaluation that is needed to get into the top mark band.

### Examiners' notes

Crime statistics are a useful example to illustrate the competing views on official statistics. The British Crime Survey is also a useful example to use in questions about surveys and questionnaire research.

### Essential notes

Marxists argue that official statistics are distorted by the powerful (e.g. they believe governments define unemployment in such a way as to reduce the figures). Introduce this third perspective to gain more evaluation and analysis marks.

### Examiners' notes

Always remember to include a short conclusion for 16-mark AS questions and a longer one for 30-mark A-level questions. Base it on the evidence and arguments put forward in your answer to show the examiner that you have thought about the issues and made a reasoned judgement about the question.

## Qualitative sources and documents

Qualitative sources are any sources with non-statistical content. They may be historical or contemporary and include:

- **public documents** – for example, transcripts of proceedings in Parliament, statements issued by companies
- **private documents** – for example, emails, paintings, song recordings, diaries and letters.

## Historical sources

These are vital for studying long-term social changes.

- Max Weber (1958) used religious tracts to study the relationship between religious belief and the development of capitalism.
- Peter Laslett (1972, 1977) used parish records to show that **industrialization** led to an increase in extended family households in Britain.

However, a problem with all historical sources is that only a proportion will survive and there is no guarantee that they are representative. In particular, there tend to be few surviving documents produced by individuals, so that often the data that sociologists would like is not available. Also, qualitative sources reflect the subjective views of those who produced them. Nevertheless this is sometimes useful, as in Weber's work.

## Life documents

**Life documents** are private documents created by individuals, which record subjective states. They include diaries, letters, photos, biographies, memoirs, suicide notes, films and pictures. Thomas and Znaniecki (1919) used letters and statements to study Polish peasants who emigrated to the USA.

Plummer (1982) argues that personal documents are rarely used by contemporary sociologists because

- surviving documents may not be representative
- they are open to differing interpretations
- they are highly subjective
- the content may be influenced by the identity of the person or people intended to read the document (except in documents intended to remain private).

However, Plummer still sees them as useful because

- they allow insights into people's subjective states
- symbolic interactionists see them as revealing the personal meanings and self-concepts which they see as shaping behaviour.

## The mass media and content analysis

The mass media may be unreliable for providing factual information, but they can be useful for revealing ideological frameworks.

**Content analysis** (analysing the content of the media) tends to be a relatively cheap research method, and as media material is easily accessible there are few problems with sampling or representativeness.

There are various methods of content analysis:

**Formal content analysis:** content is classified and counted; for example, Best (1993) counted gender roles of boys and girls in children's books. It provides objective statistical data which positivists view as social facts, allowing patterns to be uncovered. However, classification of the data may be subjective and it does not directly reveal the meaning behind the content.

**Thematic analysis:** examines the message behind the portrayal of a particular topic; for example, Soothill and Walby (1991) studied rape coverage in newspapers. It makes it possible to look at the messages behind media coverage and reveal ideological bias. However, messages are open to alternative interpretations, and the audience may not interpret the content in the same way as researchers.

**Textual analysis:** involves detailed analysis of small pieces of text; for example, the Glasgow Media Group (1974) looked at the words used to describe managers and strikers. Textual analysis provides an in-depth interpretation of media content, but does not provide an overall analysis, and can be subjective.

## Problems with qualitative sources

The points below summarize the problems with qualitative secondary sources as identified by John Scott (1990):

- **authenticity** – how genuine the documents are
- **soundness** – the document may be incomplete or unreliable
- **authorship** – it may not be written by the claimed author
- **credibility** – how believable the documents are
- **sincerity** – the author may have intended to mislead the readers
- **accuracy** – author may be untruthful
- **representativeness** – how typical the document is
- **survival**, or lack of it – representative documents may not exist
- **availability**, or lack of it – researchers may not be able to access representative samples
- **meaning** – how easy it is to understand the document
- **literal understanding** – it may be difficult to read or translate
- **interpretative understanding** – there may be possible different interpretations of what the document signifies.

## The internet as a secondary source

Stuart Stein (2002) identifies particular problems in using the internet as a secondary source. There are often no editorial or review processes to ensure the validity of the data. Consequently, data needs to be used with caution.

## Conclusion

Despite the above problems, qualitative secondary sources continue to be used because of their relative accessibility, cheapness and ability to produce insights into personal life and historical processes which could not otherwise be studied.

### Essential notes

Several research projects by the Glasgow Media Group have found evidence that the UK news mass media tends to portray a pro-capitalist image of the world and to favour perspectives put forward by governments rather than by people opposed to government policies. In part this is because powerful groups are in a strong position to influence the news agenda and to have their views aired on television news.

### Examiners' notes

The problems outlined in this list can be applied to any secondary source (statistical as well as qualitative). They can be used as the basis for the evaluation of secondary sources when answering essay questions. Remember to use examples from education.

## The educational context

Research in education can involve the study of a variety of groups. These include:

- educational staff such as teachers, head teachers and lecturers
- pupils and students (the consumers of education)
- parents of school pupils.

Research may be conducted inside educational establishments, such as schools, colleges and universities, or outside those establishments, particularly when the research involves parents.

The general issues relating to research methods apply throughout; however, there are particular issues with researching in an educational context. The specific group being studied, and the context within which the study takes place, has an impact on the practical, ethical and theoretical aspects of conducting educational research.

## Research into educational staff

### Practical issues and educational staff research

- Access to educational staff may be limited by lack of time. Teachers may feel they have little time to commit to assisting with research.
- Schools are hierarchical institutions and teachers are only likely to take part in research with the permission of their line managers. This may restrict the availability of respondents.
- Senior educational staff are themselves subject to scrutiny; for example, headteachers are responsible to school governors. This may restrict their ability or willingness to take part in research.

### Ethical issues and educational staff research

- Unguarded comments by educational staff could possibly affect career progression, so it is particularly important to maintain confidentiality for staff who take part in research.
- Observation of teachers within a staffroom setting has ethical problems if all members of the teaching staff have not consented to take part in the research.

### Theoretical issues and educational staff research

- Teachers or lecturers are likely to associate the presence of an outsider in their classroom with Ofsted inspections and may act in untypical ways in order to impress the observer. This raises questions about the validity of classroom observations.
- In interview research there may be a degree of interviewer bias and teachers may give cautious answers rather than express their true opinions because they are concerned about confidentiality.
- The teaching staff put forward to take part in the research may be hand-picked by more senior staff in order to give a positive impression of the institution, making the findings unrepresentative.

# Research into pupils and students

## Practical issues and student research

- Researchers need to get approval for the research from parents and the school rather than just from the participants.
- The Department for Education or university governing body may also need to be approached for consent.
- In most circumstances researchers will need to undergo a Criminal Records Bureau check to ensure that they are suitable people to have close contact with children.
- Researchers also have to conform to the demands of the academic year so that the timing of their research is dependent on school, college or university terms, and avoiding key events such as exams.
- There are particular problems researching young pupils who may lack the skills or confidence to fill in questionnaires or answer complex questions. Research has to be designed to take account of the abilities of particular respondents and this may limit the range of information the researcher can collect.
- Researching young children can be particularly time-consuming as they have a tendency to stray from the central points of the research. This makes it potentially expensive.

## Ethical issues and student research

There are specific ethical issues with studying children since they are considered particularly vulnerable.

- The researcher must ensure that children do not suffer any psychological distress during the research.
- Research could be interpreted as harming pupils and students if it distracts them from their education and therefore potentially impedes their performance.
- The British Sociological Association's guidelines state that the consent of children should be obtained as well as that of their parents. However, there are particular problems with gaining informed consent from young participants in research since they may not fully understand the purpose of the research.
- The guidelines also state that 'Researchers should have regard for issues of child protection and make provision for the potential disclosure of abuse'.

## Theoretical issues and student research

Theoretical issues with research into the consumers of education partly depend upon their age.

- Educational consumers of all age-groups in schools, colleges and universities occupy relatively low-status positions. They have little power, which may make it difficult for them to openly express their views. This could affect the validity of their responses.
- There may be problems with young children expressing abstract ideas or understanding questions based upon those ideas, thereby making the validity of the data open to question.

**Examiners' notes**

The best answers will cover practical, ethical and theoretical issues. Think through the process of conducting research on the topic specified in the question and try to work out what the particular problems of doing that research might be.

☞ This topic continues on the next two pages

- In observation of classrooms, the presence of the observer may well produce unnatural behaviour.
- Since access to children is dependent upon the willingness of parents and teachers to allow researchers to question them, the representativeness of a sample could be compromised. This would make it difficult to generalize from the findings of the research.

## Research into parents

### Practical issues and parent research

Parents are not usually present in schools and other educational institutions. This makes it difficult to gain access for research purposes.

- There are practical data-protection issues in getting details of parental addresses and finding ways to approach them to secure their cooperation.
- Researching parents using interviews can be time-consuming, since each home will have to be visited separately at a time that is convenient to the parents, who may well be working during the day.
- Researchers are unlikely to be able to observe the behaviour of parents when they are discussing education with their children or assisting them with homework, since this takes place in private family settings, which are not accessible to researchers.

### Ethical issues and parent research

Researching parents is much less ethically problematic than researching pupils, since parents can give properly informed consent.

The general ethical issues concerning research still apply, such as the problem of maintaining confidentiality.

### Theoretical issues and parent research

There are particular problems in obtaining a representative sample of parents.

- Parents who may be more willing to take part in research than others will tend to be those who are more involved with their children's education. Therefore research data might exaggerate the degree to which parents assist children with homework or take an interest in their schooling.
- If questionnaires are used, then there may be an uneven response-rate from different groups of parents affecting the representativeness of the data.
- Parents may also feel that they need to create a good impression to the researcher by appearing actively interested in their children's schooling and homework. This may affect the validity of any responses.

## The influence of perspectives on educational research

Although practical and ethical issues have a strong impact on the type of educational research that is carried out, **Table 19** shows how the theoretical perspective of the sociologist is also influential.

| Perspective | Focus of research and example | Main advantages | Main problems |
|---|---|---|---|
| Functionalist | The positive contribution of education to society<br><br>Example: Parsons (1961) on the functions of education | Relates education to the wider social structure | Based on abstract reasoning and not backed up by empirical evidence |
| Marxist/neo-Marxist | The way in which education serves the interests of ruling classes<br><br>Example: Bowles and Gintis (1976) studied the hidden curriculum in the USA using questionnaire research. Paul Willis (1977) studied anti-school subculture using observation and interviews | Highlights educational inequality in the context of social structure and wider inequality<br><br>Uses variety of methods to reveal this | Tends to emphasize class inequalities to the exclusion of other types (e.g. gender and ethnicity) |
| Social democratic | Class disadvantage in the education system<br><br>Example: Halsey's (1977) statistical research into class differences in achievement | Provides evidence for changes in the education system (introduction of comprehensives).<br><br>Relies largely on official statistics | Tends to have a narrow focus and neglects gender and ethnicity |
| Feminist | Patriarchal power and the education system<br><br>Example: Stanworth's (1987) research into patriarchal power and sexism in a sixth form using interviews | Moves beyond concentration on class inequality and demonstrates the existence of sexism in education | May be dated, as doesn't take account of girls overtaking boys in the education system<br><br>Whatever method is used, tends to have a narrow focus |
| Interpretivist | Classroom interaction, self-concepts, labelling and subcultures<br><br>Example: Mac an Ghaill's (1994) study of boy's subcultures in secondary schools using participant observation and interviews | Based on direct observation of actual behaviour in schools and helps to reveal the meaning of schooling for those involved<br><br>High on validity | Most interpretivist studies based on the subjective interpretations of researchers and neglect the wider social structure<br><br>Low on reliability |

**Table 19**
Influence of perspectives on educational research

The theoretical approach affects the type of data collected. Generally, structural approaches such as functionalism and Marxism tend to rely more on secondary sources for a wider analysis of the role of education in society. Interpretivists and feminists focus more on organization and processes within schools. Positivists favour quantitative methods such as questionnaires and using official statistics as secondary sources.

**Essential notes**

There are exceptions to this general correlation between perspectives and focus – some structural approaches try to link processes inside and outside schools; for example, Paul Willis' 1977 study of the anti-school subculture (see pp 8–9).

## Experimental research in education

Experimental research into the education system has been limited. However, there have been several high-profile research experiments concerned with labelling theories of education and the effects of teachers' expectations on pupil performance.

- Rosenthal and Jacobson (1968) gave false information to primary school teachers in the USA about the IQ of pupils. They found that regardless of what a pupil's actual IQ was, those who were believed by teachers to have a high IQ made greater progress than those who were believed to have a low IQ. This suggested that the self-fulfilling prophecy was occurring.
- Harvey and Slatin (1976) used photographs of children from different social classes and asked teachers to rate their likely performance in education. Pupils from higher classes were seen as more likely to be successful than pupils from lower social classes, suggesting that labelling on the basis of appearance does take place.

### Key study

#### Jane Elliott: An experiment in discrimination

Jane Elliott, a primary school teacher in Iowa in the USA, conducted an experiment in 1968 in which she deliberately discriminated in her classroom. On the first day of the experiment, she told brown-eyed children that they were inferior to blue-eyed children. She gave the blue-eyed children extra playtime, and lots of positive feedback and encouragement while the behaviour of the brown-eyed children was persistently interpreted negatively and punished. On the second day, the discrimination was reversed so that the brown-eyed children were favoured. Whichever group of children was positively labelled on a particular day, they performed much better on tests in class, and visibly displayed much more enthusiasm for schooling. The experiment led to temporary feelings of hostility between the two groups of children.

## Issues with experimental research in education

### Practical issues and experimental research

Laboratory experiments are very difficult to conduct because of the problems in gaining permission to conduct experiments and take children out of the school environment. These formal types of experiments are usually confined to studying older students rather than young children.

- The research by Harvey and Slatin was a type of laboratory experiment but was conducted on teachers rather than pupils.
- Field experiments such as those by Rosenthal and Jacobson and Elliott are more practical, but it may still be difficult to get permission from schools and teachers.

### Ethical issues and experimental research

There are major ethical problems in conducting the types of experiments described above, particularly if they involve school pupils. The research by

Rosenthal and Jacobson may have damaged the educational progress of some pupils who were labelled as having low ability. The research by Elliott led to divisions between the children within the school. In neither case was informed consent possible.

### Theoretical issues and experimental research

Experiments, which by their very nature involve the creation of artificial situations, can lack validity. Attempts to reproduce the Rosenthal and Jacobson study have produced inconsistent results, suggesting that such research may not be very reliable.

## Questionnaire research in education

**Questionnaire** research has been used in a wide variety of contexts, including the impact of parental attitudes to achievement (J.W.B. Douglas, 1964), the impact of **class** on cultural capital and achievement (Sullivan, 2001) and the choice of higher educational institution (Reay et al., 2005).

### Key study

**Alice Sullivan: Class, cultural capital and achievement**

Alice Sullivan (2001) collected data from 465 pupils in four schools, using questionnaires. She asked questions about: parents' educational qualifications, the involvement of the children in cultural activities (for example, reading books, attending the theatre and concerts) and their own educational achievements. Sullivan found a link between the performance in GCSEs and having high levels of cultural capital. She also found that cultural capital was strongly linked to class background. Her conclusion was that parental income helps to boost the educational performance of children independent of cultural factors.

### Practical issues and questionnaire research

Questionnaires make it possible to gather large amounts of information quickly and cheaply in educational settings. This type of research is relatively easy to conduct because of the existence of sampling frames such as lists of pupils and staff. It is also relatively easy to access large numbers of suitable respondents concentrated in one place. However, researchers are limited in the questions that they can put to young children or others with poor literacy skills.

### Ethical issues and questionnaire research

The main ethical problem is maintaining anonymity of respondents. There may also be a problem with getting truly informed consent from young children.

### Theoretical issues and questionnaire research

The dominance of peer groups may influence the types of answers that pupils give.

It might be difficult to prevent discussion among pupils so that they may end up collaborating on the responses. Children may be prone to making up misleading answers. This can undermine the validity of questionnaire findings.

### Examiners' notes

Don't forget to mention some advantages of this type of research as well. For example, the research is easy to replicate, making it relatively easy for other researchers to check Rosenthal and Jacobson's findings. However, as the results have been mixed, it is difficult to reach definite conclusions.

### Examiners' notes

This research is also useful for answering questions on differential achievement and social class. Remember that studies can be used both in the context of methodology questions and questions on education.

### Essential notes

Questionnaires can be distributed to a large number of schools, giving a larger sample. By contrast, observational research or interviews are limited to one school at a time.

## The use of interviews

Interviews have been used to study a wide range of educational topics. For example:

- Paul Willis (1977) used group interviews with the 'lads' who formed an anti-school subculture to understand their attitudes towards school, other pupils, teachers and careers.
- Stephen Frosh et al. (2002) used interviews with 78 boys in secondary school to collect data on their attitudes towards masculinity and how this affected their educational progress.

### Key study

#### Willam Labov: Linguistic ability

William Labov (1973) used interviews with young black American children to investigate whether children from disadvantaged backgrounds had poor language skills. In the first set of interviews they were asked questions in a formal setting by a white interviewer. In the second set they were interviewed in a formal setting by a black interviewer, and in the third, in an informal setting, by a black interviewer. In the third setting the children were able to talk fluently, whereas in the first two their language was stilted.

### Practical issues and interviews

- Interviewing children in schools requires consent from head-teachers and parents. This may limit access and those in authority may wish to restrict the scope of the interview.
- Interviewers may also be required to undergo a Criminal Records Bureau check.
- Interviews need to be carefully designed to take into account children's less developed language skills and shorter attention span. Questions therefore need to be phrased in simple language and the interview should be kept short.

However, interviews are a practical research method and it is possible to question children on a very wide range of subjects.

### Ethical issues and interviews

- Interviews with children must be carefully designed so that they do not cause distress or fatigue. They should therefore be short and avoid issues that may be sensitive.
- The confidentiality of interviews needs to be assured, although if the interview reveals evidence of abuse, interviewers have a duty to report it, thus compromising confidentiality.

### Theoretical issues and interviews

- As the study by Labov demonstrates, the validity of interview responses may be affected by the way in which the interview is conducted and by interviewer bias.
- Interviewees may see the interviewer as an authority figure, like a teacher or school inspector, and therefore be unwilling to give full and frank answers.

- Group interviews risk the responses being influenced by peer group pressure, although they may also be useful for drawing out the shared values of groups of pupils, which individuals might be reluctant to express (for example, Paul Willis's study).

## Observation and participant observation

### The uses of observational methods

Observational methods have been used widely in studying education, particularly non-participant observation. Some sociologists have conducted structured observation using the Flanders Interaction Analysis Categories (FIAC), which classify interaction in classrooms into one of 10 types and allow researchers to time the frequency and length of different types of interaction. Most observation is carried out in a less structured way; for example David Hargreaves (1967) observed teachers and pupils in secondary school without using a formal structure.

### Key study

**Devine: Observational research with primary-school children**

Devine (2003) observed classrooms and playgrounds in three primary schools in Ireland. She made sure that she sat at desks with the children and never reported misbehaviour. She stayed in the playgrounds during breaks and avoided mixing too much with teachers so that she could better understand the schools from the children's point of view.

### Practical issues in participant observation and observation

Issues of access can result from the need to obtain permission to carry out research. The role of the observer is problematic in schools, since the researcher is likely to be older than the children being observed. Observational research is likely to be time-consuming and therefore expensive, and there are practical issues about when and how field notes are recorded. Structured observation, however, makes it easier to record large amounts of standardized data.

### Ethical issues in participant observation and observation

Covert observation by adults of children is unlikely to be seen as ethically acceptable. Researchers may face ethical dilemmas if they become aware of rule-breaking behaviour by children, and they may have to put confidentiality above disclosure. If such behaviour is discussed in the research report, it is important to guarantee anonymity in the research report.

### Theoretical issues in participant observation and observation

The validity of observational research in education may be compromised by the **Hawthorne effect**. It may be impossible for researchers to blend into the background. Teachers and pupils may act unnaturally with the observer present; and the characteristics of the researcher, such as their age or ethnic group, might affect the results.

However, observation could be seen as more valid than other methods since it involves actual behaviour in real social settings.

**Examiners' notes**

Make your own additional notes on any examples of research using interviews. Examiners will be impressed if you are familiar with studies using the specified method on the particular topic.

**Essential notes**

When Hargreaves talked to some of the pupils, they told him that their teachers acted quite differently from normal when they were being observed.

**Examiners' notes**

Discussing theoretical issues is particularly important for scoring high marks.

**Essential notes**

Studies that rely mainly on unstructured observation or participant observation tend to reflect the interpretivist approach to research methods.

Always relate your comments to the specific area of education highlighted in the question. Differential achievement, gender and subject choice and issues such as school attendance, exclusions or truancy might feature.

**Essential notes**

Where particular statistics are not produced as a matter of course, then sociologists have to rely on occasional survey research carried out by the government or other bodies. For example, data on ethnicity tends to be taken from the Youth Cohort Study. This makes comparisons over time more difficult, and because the data is based on a sample it is not as reliable as data produced by every school.

**Essential notes**

School league tables are a particularly contentious issue. The Labour government introduced Contextual Value Added (CVA) tables to take into account the background of pupils when judging school performance. However, the coalition government's White Paper of 2010 led to the abolition of these types of league table.

## The use of official statistics

Official statistics are very widely used in the study of education, particularly statistics about levels of attainment and subject choice. Statistics on truancy and school exclusions as well as transitions to work and higher education are also used in educational research. These statistics are particularly useful for examining longer-term trends and making comparisons between social groups.

### Key study

**Modood: Ethnicity, class and attainment**

In a study of the relationship between ethnicity, class and attainment, Modood (2004) examined data on the proportion of pupils achieving five or more GCSE at grades A*–C in different ethnic groups. He examined data on pupils who were eligible for free school meals, and therefore from low-income families, with data on those who were not eligible. This enabled him to review the effects of income and ethnicity on achievement. He found that in all ethnic groups, pupils eligible for free school meals did less well than those who were not, but the effects of having a lower-income were much greater for white British pupils than other ethnic groups.

### Practical issues and official statistics

Official statistics are an easily accessible and plentiful source of information on education. However, the information required by sociological researchers is not always available.

Data on achievement is usually broken down into the performance of males and females, but data on class backgrounds or the ethnicity of pupils and their achievement is less often available.

Official statistics do not always use the categories that sociologists use. For example, official definitions of social class do not always match sociological definitions, so sociologists sometimes have to use indirect indicators of class, particularly whether children are receiving free school meals (FSM) or not. However, these statistics are misleading because not all of those eligible apply and, in any case, income level is not a direct measure of class.

### Ethical issues and official statistics

There are no real ethical issues in using official statistics, since they are publicly available and using them is unlikely to cause harm.

### Theoretical issues and official statistics

Official statistics tend to be comprehensive, since it is often mandatory for state-funded organizations to produce them; they are also generally reliable since the government imposes definitions and categories on educational institutions and stipulates that data is produced using standardized procedures.

However, the validity of statistics may be open to question. For example, schools may deliberately manipulate data in order to secure funding, a favourable inspection report or success in league tables. Two examples of this are when schools do not accurately record absences or lateness, or they exclude or fail to enter poorly performing pupils for exams to improve league-table performance.

## Qualitative secondary sources in education

Sociologists can make use of a wide range of public documents relating to education. These include inspection reports, school policies and publicity brochures and the minutes of governors' meetings.

They also sometimes make use of personal documents such as written work, school reports on individual pupils, or notes passed in class.

### Key study

#### Hey: Girls and friendship in education

Hey (2007) investigated friendship networks among girls in a secondary school using the notes that girls passed to one another during lessons. (She picked these notes out of the bin at the end of the lesson.) This allowed her to access the subjective views of girls, and build up a picture of their friendship networks, without using conventional methods such as interviews in which the honesty of the responses might be open to question.

### Practical issues and qualitative secondary sources

Public documents tend to be easily available to researchers and are relatively cheap and quick to access, while personal documents are not available in such large quantities, nor are they necessarily easy to access, so relatively little research has been done using them.

### Ethical issues and qualitative secondary sources

Public documents are already in the public domain, but when using private documents, ethical issues become more significant. The researcher may need to seek informed consent from those who produced the documents. If they fail to do so, then the research could be considered unethical (for example, Hey's picking private documents out of bins).

Some documents, such as school reports, could be considered to be confidential, and researchers should try to maintain the anonymity of pupils to whom they refer.

### Theoretical issues and qualitative secondary sources

The validity of public documents may be open to question; some schools would not accept that inspection reports provide a valid assessment of the school.

School publicity material is likely to put a positive gloss on the school's image and performance, while documents produced for the government by schools may be manipulated to maximize funding or increase the likelihood of positive inspection reports.

Private documents have the potential to provide valid information on the subjective viewpoints of those involved in education. However, if they are intended to be read by someone else, they may be written in a way which has the audience in mind rather than being a completely valid account.

### Essential notes

Quite a number of studies that use primary research methods supplement them with some analysis of documents. For example, in a study of the introduction of markets into education by Stephen Ball et al. (1994), extensive use was made of documents such as admissions policies and marketing material, as well as interviews with parents, in order to understand how the education market worked. Documents such as these can help a sociologist to understand the social policy context in which interaction takes place within schools.

### Examiners' notes

Discuss the validity and reliability of sources in any questions on this topic. Use your general understanding of the theoretical issues surrounding secondary sources, and apply it to the particular educational topic you are asked to discuss.

# General tips for AS Sociology Paper 1, Education with Methods in Context

## The paper as a whole

The AQA *Education with Methods in Context* for AS paper (719/1) consists of six compulsory questions that have to be completed in one of a half hours, or 90 minutes. A total of 60 marks are available for this paper, which leaves you with an average of 1.5 minutes per mark. Of these marks, 20 are for the *Methods in Context* question, and the remaining 40 are for the *Education* questions. Try to avoid spending too long on the short questions (the first three questions are worth 2 marks, 2 marks and 6 marks respectively) to leave yourself slightly more time for the longer questions. It is possible to gain full marks on the short questions without writing too much, so they should be answered concisely. You need to write in continuous prose for the 10-mark *Education* question (question 4), the 20-mark *Education* question (question 5) and the 20-mark *Methods in Context* question (question 6).

The following explanations give more detail about what you should expect from each question on the paper and how to achieve high marks.

### Education section

- **Question 01** is worth **2 marks**. This will ask you **to define** a term. You will get both marks if you give a satisfactory definition, but only 1 out of 2 if you give a partial definition or an example. If you are asked to define a subculture and you give the answer, 'A group within a wider culture, which has significantly different norms attitudes values and lifestyles to other groups in society', you would get both marks. If you give the answer 'a group such as Goths', you wouldn't have explained the term, just given an example, so you would be given 1 mark. A single sentence is usually enough to provide a definition and you shouldn't need to use more than two sentences.

  Always have a go at this question. If you include an example, you will have more chance of picking up one or both marks, even if you are not sure about your definition. Remember that there is a glossary at the back of this book which contains some key educational terms. Learning the definitions of these should prepare you well for this question.

- **Question 02** is also worth **2 marks**. It will ask you **to explain** something briefly, using an example. Although this is a short-answer question, you need to explain your example fully to achieve the full 2 marks. For example, it could ask you to explain how labelling could affect educational achievement. The example you give can be general – it doesn't need to be taken from a particular study. You might write, 'Being labelled as a troublemaker at school could lead to someone being placed in a lower set.' [1 mark for this example] 'This might result in the person losing belief in their ability and working less hard.' [1 mark for this explanation] So you need to explain *how* and *why* the example has the effect mentioned in the question.

  This is slightly more complicated than answering question 01 and we advise you to write two sentences for this to increase your chances of gaining both marks. If you are unsure about your example and explanation, you can always put a second example and explanation down and the examiner will mark positively, choosing the answer which gains you the most marks. Be mindful of time, however – remember that you should only spend a maximum of 3 minutes on each 2-mark question.

- **Question 03** will ask you **to outline three things:** for example, three ways in which schooling might be patriarchal. Fairly obviously, there are 2 marks for outlining each of the answers and you will get 2 marks for each appropriate reason that is successfully outlined, but 1 mark for a reason that is only partially outlined. So, if you are asked to outline three ways in which schooling might be patriarchal, you would get 1 mark for saying that the teaching of history could be gender-biased, and gain another mark for explaining that this is because men might feature much more than women in the history curriculum. The second part of your answer needs to provide the explanation to go with the identification of the example in the first part. If you aren't sure about one of your three answers, add a fourth and the examiner will credit you for the best three.

  You should not write your answer to this question as a continuous paragraph. Distinguish the different answers you give by starting a new line or labelling them, for example, a, b, c or i, ii, iii.

- **Question 04** will ask you to **Outline and explain two things,** for example two reasons for something or two factors, causes or effects of something. Thus you might be asked to 'Outline and explain two reasons for boys being more likely than girls to choose to study scientific subjects at A-level'. There are **10 marks** for this question and it is marked in mark bands with the highest band typically being worth 8–10 marks, the next 4–7, the lowest 1–3, or zero.

  To get in the top band, you need to show very good understanding and knowledge, successfully apply the material to the question and include some analysis. The analysis could take the form of a mini conclusion about what the two reasons show or perhaps some commentary on which reason is more important. For example, if you are answering the question above, which asks you to outline and explain two reasons for boys being more likely to choose scientific subjects at A-level, you might discuss the lack of female role models as science teachers and as scientists featured in the school curriculum, plus the impact of the wider occupational structure, and conclude that the latter is more important because career aspirations are likely to be paramount in shaping decisions about what A-levels to choose.

  It is essential to keep in mind the need for analysis in this answer and that you develop your points much more fully than in the first three questions. Think of it as a mini essay with two separate parts and perhaps a very short conclusion. Remember: about 15 minutes is allocated this question and the amount you write should reflect this.

- **Question 05** is worth **20 marks**, which means that you can spend 30 minutes on this, or even a little more if you have managed to answer some of the short questions quickly. This question will ask you to **apply material from an Item you are given and use your own knowledge to evaluate a viewpoint**. It will therefore be based upon an area of the sociology of education in the specification where there are differences of viewpoint. So it could be about, for example, reasons for differential achievement by class, gender or ethnicity, reasons for differences in subject choice by gender, different theoretical views about the role of education, different views on the effectiveness of educational policies, and so on.

Like other longer questions, this is marked using mark bands and your aim should be to get as high up as you can in the highest mark bands you can get into.

The top mark band gains you 17–20 marks and for this you will be expected to have detailed knowledge and a strong understanding, together with the use of plenty of concepts; you will have to apply your material well to the question, and be able to provide a clear and explicit evaluation of the strengths and weaknesses of different arguments, leading to a conclusion.

At a minimum, you will need to explain the viewpoint shown in the question, look at theories and/or evidence and/or arguments to support this view, do the same with other views, theories, arguments and evidence which do not support the statement, and reach a conclusion about the strengths of the arguments of the different viewpoints.

In putting together your answer, remember to include a short introduction as well as a conclusion, structure your answer clearly, include plenty of sociological content and make a logical analysis and evaluation based upon the evidence and arguments you have discussed. Ensure that you make use of the Item as well as your own knowledge. It is well worth mentioning the Item early on to make sure that you do not forget to do this. Ideally, you should make use of the Item on several occasions. Remember not to stray from the question set, and to make it clear to the examiner how your answer relates the question by referring back to it at regular intervals.

### *Methods in Context* section

- **Question 06**, the final question, is also worth **20 marks** and the same basic principles for essay writing discussed in relation to question 05 apply. As with Question 04, you are given an Item and you have to use the Item and your own knowledge to develop your response. So, a typical question will ask you **to apply material from an Item and use your own knowledge of research methods to evaluate the strengths and limitations of a method to study a particular educational topic.** As a *Methods in Context* question, you have to use your knowledge from both the study of research methods and the study of education. Even though research methods as a separate topic only appears on Paper 2 at AS level, you need to revise research methods before taking this exam so that you have the knowledge to apply your understanding of research to the educational context. The research method you could be asked about might be questionnaires, interviews, participant observation or non-participant observation, experiments, official statistics or qualitative secondary sources (e.g. documents). The question may be more specific (e.g. specifying unstructured interviews rather than interviews in general). You might be asked to discuss a wide range of educational topics. To give just a few examples, these might be unauthorised pupil absences, gender and subject choice, parental attitudes to education, the formation of pupil subcultures and so on.

Like other longer questions, this question is marked using mark bands and to get into the highest band (17–20), you need to use material from the Item and your own knowledge, demonstrate a strong knowledge and understanding of research methods, apply this to the specific educational context, evaluate by looking at both strengths and weaknesses, and reach a reasoned conclusion. In discussing the strengths and weaknesses of using a particular method in a particular educational context, you can think about *practical issues* (e.g. time, money and access), *ethical issues* (e.g. gaining informed consent and avoiding harm) and *theoretical issues* (e.g. questions of validity, reliability representativeness and generalisability). Discussing the theoretical issues is particularly important and you are unlikely to get into the highest mark band if you only discuss practical issues. It is helpful to think about any issues raised by studying the group specified in the question (e.g. pupils, teachers or parents) and the context in which the study takes place (e.g. in schools or out of schools).

Try to think through how the sort of research you are asked to write about would actually take place and apply the general issues relating to research methods to that context. For example, if you are interviewing parents about their attitudes to education in their own homes, would you get more valid answers than if you are asking them to fill in a questionnaire at school? Would the sample be more representative if you handed out questions at a parents evening or if you sent out questionnaires to parents' homes? How truthful would the answers be or how natural would the behaviour be in the particular context in which the study takes place?

The more specific you can be to the method, the way the method is being applied and the educational topic being studied, the more you are likely to impress the examiner and gain application marks. If you only give general comments about the advantages and disadvantages of a particular method with little reference to education, you will not get a high grade. If you could apply it to education more generally, you will do a little better but if you successfully apply the answer to the particular type of study, you should do very well indeed.

# Education with Methods in Context (sample AS exam Paper 1)

## Education questions

**01** Define the term 'hidden curriculum'. [**2 marks**]

**02** Using **one example**, briefly explain how gender differences in subject choice occur. [**2 marks**]

**03** Outline **three ways** in which greater parental choice has been introduced into secondary education. [**6 marks**]

**04** Outline and explain **two reasons** for the labelling of pupils. [**10 marks**]

**05** Read **Item A** below and answer the question that follows.

> ### Item A
>
> On average, higher social classes continue to perform better in the educational system and achieve higher qualifications than lower social classes, but sociologists do not agree about the reasons for this. Some argue that the main factor is cultural differences between social classes, with higher classes having a culture which equips them with the knowledge, skills and attitudes to succeed in education and that the lower social classes are in comparison culturally deprived. However, other sociologists believe that material factors such as low income and class bias within schools themselves are more important.

Applying material from **Item A** and your own knowledge, evaluate the view that differences in educational achievement between social classes are largely the result of cultural factors. [**20 marks**]

## Methods in Context question

**06** Read **Item B** below and answer the question that follows.

> ### Item B
>
> Pupils are not just passive recipients of education but actively develop their own responses to the education system. One way in which they do this is through the formation of subcultures which can be based around class, ethnicity, gender or other social divisions. The values of subcultures can have a significant effect on how positive or oppositional pupils are towards school. Unstructured interviews are a common way of studying subcultures because it may be impossible for adult researchers to join the subcultures of young people and because questionnaires are unlikely to provide an in-depth understanding of relationships in subcultures. However, it is questionable how far interview data on school subcultures provides valid data.

Applying material from **Item B** and your own knowledge of research methods, evaluate the strengths and limitations of using unstructured interviews to study different types of pupil subculture in school. [**20 marks**]

## Grade C answers

**01** *Define the term 'hidden curriculum'.* **[2 marks]**

> The hidden curriculum is where you learn things at school that you're not actually taught in lessons, e.g. that men are more powerful than women.

> This is a fairly basic answer and the explanation could be clearer and more developed. However, it does identify the essential meaning of the term 'hidden curriculum' and gives an appropriate example so it just manages to gain both marks.
> **[Mark: 2/2]**

**02** *Using **one example**, briefly explain how gender differences in subject choice occur.* **[2 marks]**

> Girls might choose more creative or literacy based subjects and boys more practical and physical subjects like PE and DT. This might be because they label these subjects as male or female and this could happen because of the gender of the teachers teaching these subjects.

> This answer works well. An example is provided and connected points are made in a well-reasoned way to explain how the gender differences occur. There is a reference to a sociological concept (label) and this response gains both marks quite efficiently providing the minimum required.
> **[Mark: 2/2]**

**03** *Outline **three ways** in which greater parental choice has been introduced into secondary education.* **[6 marks]**

> Greater parental choice has been introduced by:
>
> 1. Parents don't have to worry about catchment areas anymore and can send their children to the school they most like.
>
> 2. Parents also have more choice because there are more types of schools to choose, like Free schools and different types of academy.
>
> 3. Parents can make better choices now, because they will know about the schools because of more publicity like websites and Ofsted Reports.

> This answer is laid out well and has identified three ways in which there might be greater parental choice. The first reason though is flawed because catchment areas are still important – where you live remains a crucial factor as to whether you get into most oversubscribed schools – although you can apply to schools which are outside your local area. The point is not fully explained and would

therefore get 1 mark out of 2. The second point is clearly a valid one. The student has named two new types of school, illustrating the point that there is now more choice so this would get 2 out of 2. The third point starts off suggesting that 'better choices' can be made, which is not quite the same as providing more choice. However, it also makes the point that parents will know about more schools, which would facilitate having more choice. This is not fully explained so the student would get 1 mark out of 2.

**[Mark: 4/6]**

---

**04** *Outline and explain **two reasons** for the labelling of pupils.* **[10 marks]**

Students might be labelled because of their working-class culture. Working-class pupils have lower achievement at school, and this might be caused by them having cultural deprivation. They might not have experienced a wide variety of things or places. This might mean that in lessons these students sometimes appear to be less academic, as they won't know things the middle-class students know. Also they might not have the same attitudes to education and studying. This might mean that teachers will label them as not being as intelligent or interested in the lessons. Once they'd been labelled like this, then teachers will spend less time helping them, or see them in a negative way and the self-fulfilling prophecy will mean that this label becomes true. Howard Becker did a study on teacher labelling and found that teachers saw middle-class students as 'ideal', so they were labelling on their class.

Students might also be labelled because of their gender. Attainment results show that girls tend to do better in school. This might be because of being labelled. Girls might be seen as better, more obedient and more intelligent students. Boys might be seen as less focused, mature and more likely to disrupt. There is evidence like the Paul Willis study which shows a negative working-class lads culture. These lads weren't interested in school and would have been labelled negatively.

In both parts of this answer, the student has identified possible reasons for labelling – one based on class and one on gender. The first part of the answer is more developed than the second: some sociological concepts are used and a reasonable understanding is demonstrated. The answer is not applied terribly well to the question in places; in one sentence the student talks more about the attitudes of the pupil than the reasons why they are labelled. One study is referenced, but there was scope to include more sociological content in the discussion of why teachers might negatively label working-class pupils. For example, there could have been discussion of the culture clash between the culture of teachers with the culture of working-class pupils and Bourdieu's views on cultural capital could have been usefully mentioned to show how cultural differences led to labelling.

The second part of the answer is less well-developed and doesn't have a very clearly reasoned explanation for why girls are seen as better. It is implied that this might be because girls are 'better' in terms of their achievement and this wouldn't really fit with the idea of gender bias. One study is mentioned (Paul Willis) but this study wasn't really about labelling as such so it provides weak evidence. Overall, this is a moderate answer that is relatively weak in terms of application and analysis.

**[Mark: 5/10]**

**05** *Applying material from **Item A** and your own knowledge, evaluate the view that differences in educational achievement between social classes are largely the result of cultural factors.* **[20 marks]**

There is evidence to show that culture will affect how well you achieve at school. If you are culturally deprived, you might have been brought up with different opinions and attitudes towards school than someone who is middle class. If your parents are manual workers, they may not see school as important as someone whose parents have professional jobs like a doctor. For middle-class children whose parents are professional, there may be an expectation that they will do well at school, as education will be seen as important. Paul Willis's study showed the working-class 'lads' were expecting to follow their fathers by working in factories. This meant that school wasn't important and so they didn't try and were actually disruptive. Children from these backgrounds might find they don't see education as important and are more interested in immediate gratification than going to university.

Linguistic deprivation as Bernstein researched, was also an issue related to class and part of cultural deprivation. Working-class families spoke in the restricted code at home, and so this was the only speech code their children could use. This would make it more difficult for students to understand textbooks, exam papers and even the teacher, as teachers will use the elaborate code. Middle-class children will be able to use both, as their parents are more likely to be better educated. They will use the elaborate code at home and so will have a good understanding of what is being discussed in lessons.

There are other factors that will affect educational achievement. Material deprivation and home life will also affect things because students (due to a parent's lack of money) may have few resources at home, e.g. computer, revision books or even a desk and space to work at. This might mean they can't complete homework easily or there's a lack of space and overcrowding, which could make concentrating difficult. Harker looked at material deprivation and found that it led to mental health issues, bullying and days off school, so this would affect results.

School factors such as teacher labelling would affect educational differences. If someone from a lower class is negatively labelled because of their class, as Howard Becker found that middle-class students tended to be seen as ideal, this could mean that working-class students are more likely to be treated differently. This might make them even more negative about school and education and would lead to the self-fulfilling prophecy. Finally, school may not seem that relevant and may cause some students to switch off. It might be seen as training you more for an academic career. Some students will not see this as relevant.

This paragraph demonstrates a sound but quite basic understanding of some aspects of cultural deprivation, focused particularly on attitudes towards school. The range of issues discussed is fairly limited and not particularly conceptually detailed. The paragraph could have linked in issues such as attitudes towards deferring or seeking immediate gratification, individualistic or collectivist attitudes, and more specifically about lacking the knowledge required to succeed in education. One useful example is included but it would have been even more useful to have referenced more contemporary research.

This paragraph provides a useful description and application of Bernstein's ideas on speech codes but the explanation of the different types of speech codes could be more developed.

This paragraph includes some basic analysis and evaluation. The student successfully identifies an alternative interpretation of differential achievement. It links well with the Item's discussion of material factors and offers some alternative explanation but is fairly basic in terms of its development.

As in the previous paragraph, an alternative explanation for differential achievement is presented, although the comparison is implicit. The student does not directly use this material to criticise cultural deprivation theories. If they had done so, the analysis and evaluation would have been stronger.

Overall, this answer provides quite a basic outline of a successful response to the question but it doesn't score very highly in terms of any of the skills. The knowledge is limited and the understanding is quite superficial. Application to the question is weak in places. No direct mention is made of the Item, some of the material is only implicitly related to the question and is more concerned with class in general than cultural deprivation in particular. The analysis is limited and much of the evaluation is made through stating different views rather than analysing the differences between them (examiners call this 'juxtaposition' – a classic weakness of some less strong answers). There is scope to improve in all these areas. This would place the answer in lower end of the 9–12 mark band.

**[Mark: 9/20]**

---

A vague start. It would be more useful to give a brief definition of subcultures and of unstructured interviews, but application is demonstrated through the reference to the question.

06 *Applying material from **Item B** and your own knowledge of research methods, evaluate the strengths and limitations of using unstructured interviews to study different types of pupil subculture in school.* **[20 marks]**

Unstructured interviews could be a good way of finding out about student subcultures, although as Item B says, it might be more successful depending on the type of subculture.

If a sociologist was looking at an anti-school subculture, an unstructured interview would be better than a questionnaire due to literacy skills and the student not being able to fully understand the questionnaire. As the student is anti-school, they might also be anti-authority. Unstructured interviews are good because you can spend a long time doing them and get to know the interviewee. This means if the student is anti-authority, hopefully they will build up a rapport and start giving more detailed answers. It would be a good idea for the interviewer to look casual rather than smartly dressed, so the group can relate to him or her more easily. This is also a disadvantage though, as it makes the method very expensive and time consuming. There is also a possibility that the student will not develop a rapport and will not be honest. Especially due to the student's position in the sub-cultural group, he or she doesn't want to be seen to be working with adults and helping them.

This is a strong paragraph in a number of ways. It is very well applied to the specific question. It draws on the particular characteristics of the group being studied (pupils in subcultures) and considers how suitable the method would be for studying the particular phenomenon (subcultures) with this group of people. Analysis and evaluation is developed by considering alternative methods. There is reasonable balance in the evaluation as both strengths and weaknesses are considered. Theoretical and practical issues are mentioned though in a somewhat superficial way at times.

Another issue with unstructured questionnaires is that they are all different as there is no interview schedule and can't be compared. This means that it might be difficult to draw firm conclusions from them. With an anti-subcultural pupil, they might like the opportunity to talk about the things they dislike about school. They may never get asked their opinion so this could be a good opportunity for them to open up, or they might just use it as an opportunity to criticise the school and teachers. This might be more likely if the interview is done as a group interview, where these students will want to impress their friends and keep their standing within the group.

This paragraph continues to discuss theoretical issues about the quality of the data likely to be produced through this type of research. There is a recognition that there are different types of unstructured interview, showing knowledge of research methods and adding a little sophistication to the discussion.

If high-achieving students are interviewed there are likely to be different issues and pressures. They might be more likely to respect and relate to authority figures and say more, they may even want to 'please' and so say answers which they see as 'socially desirable' rather than their real opinion. If the interviewer decided to do a group interview with a mixed group of students this might not work well. Those who felt more powerful and dominant would be likely to speak more and silence the others, who might feel embarrassed or undermined. As Paul Willis found, the anti-school group might laugh at and belittle the motivated and pro-school group. This would mean that the interviewer wouldn't get the full range of ideas.

Some more good points are made here. Earlier the student had assumed that those in subcultures would be anti-school, but in this paragraph there is recognition that pro-school groups might also be interviewed. However, there is some loss of focus in the application because 'subcultures' are not mentioned in this paragraph and the student is really discussing the use of unstructured interviews with pupils in a more general context. Some knowledge of the sociology of education is displayed with the Willis example, but a very limited range of knowledge about the sociology of education has been displayed in the paper as a whole.

Overall, this is stronger than the longer answers to the education questions because most of the response is well applied to the specific context and the research method. There are a number of thoughtful and perceptive points made, demonstrating the ability to analyze and evaluate. The answer could have been improved with a more systematic structure including a distinctive introduction and a distinctive conclusion. Although some of the points are linked together, there is no real organising principle behind how the essay is ordered and the student could have looked at strengths and weaknesses in separate sections or perhaps of distinguished theoretical, ethical and practical issues. Ethical issues are ignored and the addition of these would strengthen the answer. The more difficult skills of application, analysis and to a lesser extent evaluation are handled well, but knowledge is somewhat lacking. There is very limited use of technical terms concerning research methods (such as reliability, validity, generalisability) and no links are made to general approaches to methodology (such as positivism and interpretivism). A wider range of examples including some contemporary ones would also have been helpful. Although not quite good enough for the top mark band, this would still score well.

**[Mark: 14/20]**

Total marks: 2 + 2 + 2 + 4 + 5 + 9 + 14 = 36/60 = 60% = Grade C

# General tips for AS Sociology Paper 2, Research Methods

Paper 2 (7191/2) is a 90-minute paper that is worth 60 marks, so, as on Paper 1 an average of 1.5 minutes are allocated per mark. The paper is divided into two sections. The first section covers *Research Methods* and the content you need to answer this section is covered in this book. The second section covers the option topics of *Families and Households* (covered in Collins Sociology Student Support Materials AQA AS and A-level Sociology: Families and Households book ISBN 9780008221669), *Culture and Identity, Health and Work, Welfare and Poverty*. The comments that follow, therefore, only apply to the Research Methods component, which is worth **20 marks.** You should spend about 30 minutes on this question in your exam. This part of the paper consists of just two questions, one worth 4 marks and one worth 16 marks.

- **Question 07** (4 marks) will ask you to outline two things (perhaps two advantages, disadvantages, problems, criticisms, features) of a particular research method, or perhaps two factors (e.g. two ethical factors influencing the choice of method). You could be asked, for example, about participant observation, structured interviews, postal questionnaires or official statistics. For these answers, you will get 2 marks if you give a clear and accurate outline, and 1 mark if you give a partial outline. For example, if you are asked to outline two problems of using participant observation in sociological research, you will get 2 marks if you answer 'one problem of using participant observation is gaining access to the group you wish to study since the personal characteristics of the researcher may not be the same as the group you are trying to join, e.g. an older person trying to join in a youth subculture'. You will only get 1 of the 2 marks if you say 'one problem of using participant observation is access' because the explanation is not full enough to demonstrate that you fully understand the point. Therefore, as well as making the basic point, explain it; do that twice for two different problems (or whatever you are asked for) and you should gain full marks.

- **Question 08** (16 marks) is likely to ask you to 'Evaluate the problems' of using a particular research method in sociological research or to consider ethical, practical or theoretical issues in research. For example, you might be asked to 'Evaluate the problems of using official government statistics in sociological research'. As for other longer questions, this is marked in mark bands and to get into the top mark bands (13–16) you need to have detailed knowledge, use appropriate concepts, apply the material effectively to the question and have a reasonable level of evaluation or analysis. You should spend approximately 24–5 minutes on this question.

  It is always worth trying to ensure that you cover practical, ethical and theoretical problems when discussing a method and you should spend most time on theoretical issues. It is particularly useful if you can link the theoretical issues to questions of validity, reliability, representativeness and generalisability and also make links to theoretical approaches to research such as positivism and interpretivism. You might also raise issues relating to questions of possible bias and subjectivity. In terms of practical issues, you can consider time, money and access to the subjects, and in terms of ethics remember to think about whether any deceit is involved, whether it is possible to gain informed consent, maintain the anonymity of the subjects and whether anyone might be harmed in any way. Make sure that you explain or illustrate the practical, ethical or theoretical issues you raise and the inclusion of some examples can help to demonstrate your understanding and also help you demonstrate the skill of application.

Analysis in your answer could involve explaining why something is a problem or perhaps briefly mentioning ways in which you could limit or manage the problem. Evaluation can involve discussing how great a problem something is. You don't need to go into detail about the advantages of an approach if the question asked you about the problems, but it can be useful to mention from time to time that the problems have a flipside. For example, if you are discussing that questionnaires may lack validity, you might mention briefly that some sociologists believe they partially make up for this because of their reliability.

These are fairly straightforward questions and if you think about how you would answer this type of question in relation to each major type of research method, and in terms of questions about factors influencing the choice of method, you should be well prepared for the exam.

# Research Methods (sample exam Paper 2)

## Questions

**07** *Outline **two** problems with using official statistics in sociological research.* [**4 marks**]

**08** *Evaluate the problems with using questionnaires in sociological research.* [**16 marks**]

## Grade C answers

**07** *Outline **two** problems with using official statistics in sociological research.*

> 1. The figures can't always be trusted and don't show the 'true' picture, e.g. the dark figure of crime.
>
> 2. They show trends but don't give any explanations or reasons.

> The brief first part of the answer does, however, identify a problem and gives a minimal explanation of it. To be certain of securing both marks, a more developed answer with a second sentence would have been better but nevertheless just manages to gain 2 out of 2 marks. The second point gives only a partial explanation and is insufficiently developed to demonstrate a full understanding but the essence of a valid point is there (1 out of 2 marks)
> **[Mark: 3/4]**

**08** *Evaluate the problems with using questionnaires in sociological research.*

The first paragraph demonstrates competent if quite basic knowledge of the different types of questionnaire, which is useful background but there has been no discussion of 'problems' as yet.

> There are a range of different types of questionnaire. They can be open or closed, they can be face-to-face or postal/online. Open questionnaires are when the respondent is able to write in their own answers but closed ones are when there are pre-coded answers and you just tick your response. The type of questionnaire you use might depend on the type of study you are doing or the sample group that you are using.
>
> The good thing about closed questionnaires is that they are quick for people to respond to as they don't have to write long answers. This also means that the results are quick and easy to correlate and wouldn't need an expert to do it. Another good thing is that even people with low literacy might find these easy to complete. But a disadvantage is that they aren't very personal and you couldn't ask questions about sensitive topics with this method. You don't get to know your respondents, so it would be easy for them to lie and give socially desirable answers.

This paragraph starts with a discussion of the practical advantages of questionnaires before listing some disadvantages (one practical and one theoretical). There is some basic analysis and evaluation but the response is quite simplistic. The student does not apply the material to the word 'problems' in the question, does not use of technical terms and there is no real depth.

With open questionnaires more information is gathered. This might help the sociologist to find out more about their sample and find out about their feelings. But even with open questionnaires, people often don't expect to write too much and may still give socially desirable answers.

This is a stronger paragraph which uses a technical term (response rate) and it has a better focus on 'problems'. An example is included too, demonstrating application skills.

The structure of the answer becomes clearer as the student discusses different types of question. A useful concept, 'socially desirable answers', is included here but the paragraph is very short.

If the questionnaire is postal or online you can reach lots of people and send out the surveys very cheaply/for free. But there can be a problem with the response rate. This can be very low, as Hite found. Hers was 4.5%. You don't know if people understood the question or who even filled in the survey and you can often get a certain profile of respondent, e.g. female, older or unemployed. It would also be difficult to send out questionnaires for sensitive topics.

So all kinds of questionnaires have their advantaged and disadvantages, and it depends what the study is about to know whether questionnaires are suitable. They are always a problem if you want in-depth data but they can be useful for basic factual data.

The final paragraph offers a reasoned conclusion demonstrating better analytical and evaluative skills. This ties the answer together well and improves the overall mark although it is still quite basic. If the rest of the answer had been more like this but with more depth, better use of technical terms like validity and reliability with better application to the word 'problems', it would have transformed a mediocre answer into a very good one. [Mark: 9/16]

**Total marks: 3 + 9 = 12/20 = 60% = Grade C standard for this component**

# General tips for A-level Sociology Paper 1

## The paper as a whole

The AQA *Education with Theory and Methods* A-Level paper (7192/1) consists of six compulsory questions that have to be completed in 2 hours or 120 minutes. There are a total of **80** marks available for this paper, which leaves you with an average of 1.5 minutes per mark (the same as other papers). Of these marks, 50 are for the *Education* component of the paper, **20** are for the *Methods in Context* question, and the remaining **10** are for *Theory and Methods*. Try to avoid spending too long on the short questions (the first two questions are worth **4** and **6** marks respectively) in order to leave yourself as much time as possible for the longer questions. It is possible to gain full marks on the short questions without writing too much, so they should be answered concisely. You need to write in continuous prose when answering the 10-mark, 20-mark and 30-mark questions. There is a 10-mark *Education* and a 10-mark *Theory and Methods* question on the paper, a 20-mark *Methods in Context* question and a 30-mark *Education* question. (To be fully prepared for the Theory and Methods question you will need to revise the advanced theories and methods covered in the Collins Student Support Materials AQA A-level Crime and Deviance with Theory and Methods book ISBN 9780008221645.)

### Education section

- **Question 01** will ask you to **outline two things**, for example two ways in which schooling might be patriarchal. Fairly obviously, there are 2 marks for outlining each of the answers and you will get 2 marks for each appropriate reason that is successfully outlined but 1 mark for a reason only partially outlined So if you are asked to 'Outline two ways in which schooling might be patriarchal' you would get 1 mark for saying that the teaching of history could be gender-biased, and gain another mark for explaining that this is because men might feature much more than women in the history curriculum. The second part of your answer provides the explanation to go with the identification of the example in the first part. If you aren't sure about one of your two answers, add a third and the examiner will credit you for the best two. You should not write your answer to this question as a continuous paragraph, but instead distinguish the different answers you are giving by starting a new line or labelling them, for example a, and b or i and ii.

- **Question 02** will ask you to **outline three things for 6 marks,** for example to outline three reasons why some minority ethnic groups gain above-average qualifications. The marking for this works in the same way as for question 1 and the same principles therefore apply. You need to fully outline each thing, in this case each reason, and if you only partially outline an appropriate reason you will only get 1 of the marks available for each of the three points. As in question 1, clearly distinguish the different points rather than writing in continuous prose. If you are uncertain about one of your three points, you can add a fourth, so long as you don't spend too long on the question as a whole.

- **Question 03** is a **10-mark question** but is different from the 10-mark questions on AS papers. This question has an Item attached to it and the skill of application is particularly important because **you are asked to apply the material from the Item and analyse two things (they could be factors, effects, reasons or even changes)**. So you could be asked to analyze two factors that lead to high level of middle-class educational achievement, analyse two effects of particular government educational policies, two reasons why feminists see education as patriarchal or two changes in the organisation of schooling.

To answer these questions, you have to identify two points from the Item provided that are relevant to the question and then discuss them. As you have about 15 minutes to answer this question, you can produce reasonably developed answers. The discussion could focus on issues such as why they are significant and how significant they are. To get into the top mark band (8–10) you need good knowledge and understanding to be able to apply it clearly and to include analysis and evaluation. It may be worthwhile including a one- or two-sentence conclusion linking your two points and evaluating how important each of them is.

- **Question 04** is an essay question worth **30 marks**, so this is the most valuable question on the paper and should take up around 45 minutes of your time. It takes the same form as the 20-mark AS question, but you have an extra 15 minutes (45 minutes as opposed to 30 minutes at AS). You need to use this to add more depth and detail in your knowledge and understanding, and apply this consistently to the question over your whole answer, and also to develop your analysis and evaluation more. Compared with 20-mark questions, you have more time to explore contradictory arguments and to discuss all sides of a debate more fully.

This question will ask you to **apply material from an Item you are given and use your own knowledge to evaluate a viewpoint**. It will therefore be based upon an area of the sociology of education in the specification where there are differences of view. So it could be a sociological perspective on education (Marxism, feminism, neoliberalism, postmodernism or functionalism), reasons for differential achievement by class, gender or ethnicity, educational policies, different explanations of processes in schools and so on. This, like other longer questions, is marked in mark bands and your aim should be to get as high as you can in the highest mark bands you can get into. The top mark band gains you 23–30 marks and for this band you are expected to have detailed knowledge and a strong understanding with the use of plenty of concepts. You will have to apply your material well to the question, and have clear and explicit evaluation of the strengths and weaknesses of different arguments leading to a conclusion. You also need to show reasonable 'sophistication'. To give two examples, if you were discussing feminist views it is important to distinguish different types of feminism; when discussing a perspective, you need to be specific about the views of individual theorists.

As a minimum you need to explain the view in the question, look at theories and/or evidence and/or arguments to support that view, do the same with views, theories, arguments and evidence which do not support the statement, and reach a conclusion about the strengths of the arguments. Include a short introduction as well as a conclusion, structure your answer clearly, include plenty of sociological content and make the analysis and evaluation logical and based upon the evidence and arguments you have discussed. You need to ensure that you make use of the Item as well as your own knowledge, so it is well worth mentioning the Item early on to make sure that you do not forget this and ideally you should make use of the Item on at least two or three occasions. Also, remember not to stray from the question you have been set, and ensure that you make it clear to the examiner how your answer relates the question by referring back to it at regular intervals.

This question gives you the opportunity to really show off your skills, knowledge and understanding so make the most of the opportunity and make full use of everything relevant you have learned on your course. Try to demonstrate a confident command of the subject matter, apply that to the question and demonstrate the ability to argue convincingly for a particular point of view.

### *Methods in Context* section

The next question – **question 05** – is worth **20 marks** and follows the same format as the *Methods in Context* question on the AS paper. You are given an Item and have to use the Item and your own knowledge to develop your response. **Thus a typical question asks you to apply material from an Item and use your own knowledge of research methods to evaluate the strengths and limitations of a method to study a particular educational topic.** As for a *Methods in Context* question, you will have to use your knowledge taken from both the study of research methods and the study of education. The research method you could be asked about might be questionnaires, interviews, participant observation or non-participant observation, experiments, official statistics or qualitative secondary sources, (e.g. documents). The question may be more specific (e.g. specifying unstructured interviews rather than interviews in general). You might be asked to discuss a wide range of educational topics. To give just a few examples, these might be unauthorised pupil absences, gender and subject choice, parental attitudes to education, the formation of pupil subcultures and so on.

As for other longer questions, this question is marked using mark bands. To get into the highest mark band (17–20), you will need to use material from the Item and your own knowledge, demonstrate a strong knowledge and understanding of research methods, apply this to the specific educational context, evaluate by looking at both strengths and weaknesses, and reach a reasoned conclusion. In discussing the strengths and weaknesses of using a particular method in a particular educational context, you can think about *practical issues* (e.g. time, money and access), *ethical issues* (e.g. gaining informed consent and avoiding harm) and *theoretical issues* (e.g. questions of validity, reliability representativeness and generalisability). Discussing the theoretical issues is particularly important and you are unlikely to get into the highest mark band if you only discuss practical and ethical issues. It is helpful to think about any issues raised by studying the group specified in the question (e.g. pupils, teachers or parents) and the context in which the study takes place (e.g. in schools or out of schools).

Try to think through how the sort of research you are asked to write about would actually take place and apply the general issues relating to research methods to that context. For example, if you were interviewing parents about their attitudes to education in their own homes, would you get more valid answers than if you were asking them to fill in a questionnaire at school? Would the sample be more representative if you handed out questions at a parents' evening or if you sent out questionnaires to parents' homes? How truthful would the answers be or how natural would the behaviour be in the particular context in which the study takes place?

The more specific you can be to the method, the way the method is being applied and the educational topic being studied, the more you are likely to impress the examiner. If you only give general comments about the advantages and disadvantages of a particular method with little reference to education, you will not get a high grade. If you can apply your answer to education more generally you will do a little better, but if you successfully apply your answer to the particular type of study you should do very well indeed.

## *Theory and Methods* section

The final question, **question 06**, is a *Theory and Methods* question. To answer this question, you will need to have revised both the material in this book and the *Theory and Methods* material in AQA topic 4.3.2 as it is possible you could be asked about any topic in the A-level *Theory and Methods* specification. (To be fully prepared for the Theory and Methods question you will need to revise the advanced theories and methods covered in the Collins Student Support Materials AQA A-level Crime and Deviance with Theory and Methods book ISBN 9780008221645, as well as the sections in this book.)

This is a **10-mark question** so you should spend about **15 minutes** on it. This question provides you with an Item, and it follows the same format as the AS 10-mark questions, asking you to **apply material from an Item to outline and explain two things (e.g. reasons, factors, causes, ways or effects) of something**. So it could ask about two reasons that sociologists rarely use experiments or two ways in which sociology can be seen as scientific. You should answer these questions in full sentences and make sure that you distinguish two distinct points although you could tie them together at the end with a one- or two-sentence conclusion. Try to connect together linked points in discussing each of the reasons (or however the question is phrased). It can also be useful to illustrate your answer with examples.

These questions are marked using mark bands and to get into the top mark band (typically 8–10) you need to show very good understanding and knowledge, successfully apply the material to the question and include some analysis. The analysis could take the form of a mini-conclusion about what two reasons show or perhaps some commentary on which reason is more important. For example, in discussing two reasons why sociologists rarely use experiments, you might discuss practical and theoretical reasons and conclude that practical reasons are more significant because it is simply not possible to conduct experiments on many topics of interest to sociologists. It is essential to develop the reasoning in your answer, explaining each of your reasons in some detail and applying the Item rather than just stating your reasons.

## *Education with Theory and Methods* (sample exam Paper 1)
### Education questions

01  Outline **two** material factors that may affect gender differences in educational achievement.  [**4 marks**]

02  Outline **three ways** in which globalisation has affected education in the UK.  [**6 marks**]

03  Read **Item A** below and answer the question that follows.

> ### Item A
> Both Conservative and Labour governments in recent decades have introduced a whole range of different types of secondary school to increase variety in the state schooling system. The intention has been to give parents a wider choice of school. This contrasts with the comprehensive system where pupils were simply expected to go to their local comprehensive school. Parents could sometimes choose between local comprehensives, but there was no option to attend a different type of state school. Now each geographical area has a variety of different types of school that might include academies (with different characteristics), non-academy schools, free schools, and in some places grammar schools. However, while parents may have a wider variety of schools to choose from, some parents cannot always get their children into their first-choice school.

Applying material from **Item A**, analyse **two** reasons why some parents are unable to obtain places for their children in their first-choice school. [**10 marks**]

04  Read **Item B** below and answer the question that follows.

> ### Item B
> Ethnic differences in educational achievement are complex, and have changed over time. Some ethnic groups, particularly Chinese and Indian ethnic groups, consistently outperform white British ethnic groups in the British education system. Other ethnic groups, such as Bangladeshis and Pakistanis, have caught up with the performance of white British groups at GCSE level, although they did less well than

white British groups in the past. The performance of black ethnic groups in education has also improved although black boys continue do less well than the average at GCSE level. In part, these changes and patterns could be due to factors inside school, with schools becoming more effective at meeting the needs of ethnic minorities but still sometimes discriminating, intentionally or unintentionally, against black children. However, factors in the wider society may also be important.

Applying material from **Item B** and your own knowledge, evaluate the view that ethnic differences in educational achievement are mainly the result of factors inside school. [**30 marks**]

## *Methods in Context* question

05   Read **Item C** below and answer the question that follows.

### Item C

Some sociologists believe that parents have a strong influence on the educational achievement of their children because of the way that they bring their children up and their attitudes to schooling. Parents may help to equip their children with the knowledge and skills necessary to succeed in school, for example by reading to them, taking an interest in their educational progress or by emphasizing to them the importance of getting higher education qualifications. To investigate this it is often most convenient to use questionnaire research because parents are widely dispersed and may not be easily accessible to take part in interviews. Questionnaire research may be the most practical method to use because large amounts of standardised data can be collected from a large sample of the parents and can be used to produce standardised statistical data, which can then be analysed to look for correlations between parenting and achievement.

Applying material from **Item C** and your own knowledge of research methods, evaluate the strengths and limitations of using questionnaires to investigate the role of parents in producing social class differences in pupil attitudes to school. [**20 marks**]

## *Theory and Methods* question

06   Outline and explain two arguments against the view that participant observation produces valid data. [**10 marks**]

## Grade C answers

**01** *Outline **two material factors** that may affect gender differences in educational achievement.* **[4 marks]**

• Labelling and teacher expectations might affect gender differences in school. Teachers may expect more of girls and see them as more academic and boys as more disruptive and less academic.

• Also the curriculum can affect outcome as the curriculum has become more feminised with lots of reading and writing and less practical work which might not appeal so much to boys.

This is a very clear and effective answer to the question. Both points are valid ones and there is sufficient explanation to provide a full outline and to secure all the marks. The points are clearly explained and make well established sociological claims.

**[Mark: 4/4]**

**02** *Outline **three ways** in which globalisation has affected education in the UK.* **[6 marks]**

• Globalization has involved some multinational companies becoming involved in running parts of the education system, for example the exam board Edexcel. This might result in more marketization and the introduction of ideas from abroad.

• Also as the UK has lost some of its industries, these have moved abroad, e.g. the more industrial industries, so in UK schools we need to think more about international work.

• Finally British results are compared with other countries' international league tables.

The first point is valid and gains 2 out of 2 marks. Edexcel is not in itself an international company, but it is part of a bigger company (Pearson), which is. The second point focuses more on changes in work than on education and only gives a weak explanation as to how this may have impacted on the education system. This point is partially outlined and therefore gains 1 out of 2 marks. The final point also gains 1 out of 2 marks because it identifies an international comparison that is made, but doesn't really discuss the consequences for the education system such as a tendency towards 'teaching the basics' and using less student-centred learning in subjects such as maths and science.

**[Mark: 4/6]**

**03** *Applying material from **Item A**, analyse **two reasons** why some parents are unable to obtain places for their children in their first-choice school.* **[10 marks]**

The most popular schools tend to be 'oversubscribed'. This means these schools will not have enough places for all of the students who apply. When a school is oversubscribed parents can appeal for a place if they really want one, but this is difficult because there may be lots of competition for just a few spare places. Middle-class parents are most likely to be successful.

As the Item says, geographical areas have a wide variety of schools. Some of these schools might be selective, e.g. by faith or intelligence. If students cannot pass the tests or do not meet the requirements, then even if the parent wants to send the child there, they will not be able to.

This is a good start to the answer. The student demonstrates application skills by immediately referring to the Item and all the material included is relevant. Indeed, there is a good focus upon internal factors within the school. Specific research is mentioned and at the end of the paragraph there are some attempts at evaluation and analysis (although this is a little vague). The knowledge could have been more precise in that Gillborn and Youdell argue that teachers tend to concentrate on those who are marginal for achieving a C grade.

These are very competent answers, but they lack a little development. For the first point, the student could have said rather more about class differences in gaining places at over-subscribed schools by discussing the ways in which middle-class parents can manipulate the system, for example by buying houses in the catchment area for the most popular schools. In the second part of the answer, there could have been more analysis of the selective nature of some schools, for example the student could have commented on the continuation of grammar schools in some areas and given more detail on the kind of tests that are applied to determine whether a pupil gets a place. Limited use is made of the Item and the answer is a little short for this type of question. With more development, it could have got into the top mark band.
**[Mark: 6/10]**

04  *Applying material from **Item B** and your own knowledge, evaluate the view that ethnic differences in educational achievement are mainly the result of factors inside school.*  **[30 marks]**

As stated in the Item, some ethnic groups outperform white British students, others are beginning to catch up. Chinese and Indian groups are typically successful in school. This could be due to positive teacher labelling. Gillborn and Youdell suggest that teachers concentrate on the A to C economy, meaning that they are most interested in students who will reach these grades. Chinese and Indian students may be seen as hardworking and focused, so therefore will have teacher attention and support to do well. Not everyone agrees with this, as some sociologists suggest that these students are actually negatively labelled and seen as passive with a poor understanding of English. Therefore they might be ignored.

Black students who still tend to underperform may also be affected by teacher labelling. This can be for both boys and girls. There is evidence from Gillborn and Youdell who found that teachers treated black students differently and more harshly than their fellow students. They tended to punish them more quickly and harshly for the same behaviour as other students. This leads to a spiralling behaviour as black students began to feel more negatively about their teachers and education. This study is also backed up by evidence of exclusions, where black students are more likely to be internally excluded in schools and also placed in referral units. ☞

Good knowledge is demonstrated here with two studies being mentioned, both of which are relevant and, because of the differences between them, provide the opportunity for some analysis and evaluation. The application could be more directed to the question if the student had simply pointed out where internal and external factors were involved so this is a missed opportunity to demonstrate this skill.

Fuller looks at black girls, and she does agree that there is negative stereotyping, but she finds that the girls don't accept them and are more successful because of them.

Another internal factor is the language and curriculum. For some ethnic students the language will be a problem, especially if their parents are not English speaking as there will be no development of language skills at home. Literacy is a big part of every subject in the curriculum, so language can be a real disadvantage. Language can also link to labelling. If a student cannot fluently speak English, the teacher might see the student as unable. The curriculum can also be ethnocentric and not engage or interest students from other countries.

The identification of the curriculum as a possible factor is very helpful and the suggestion that it might be ethnocentric makes a good point. However, the response strays into discussing factors that are not really internal to the school: that is, the English skills of the individual pupil. If the answer had concentrated on saying that schools failed to provide adequate support for those for whom English is not their first language, it would have been able to turn this into an internal factor. However, as it is, the application is weak in some parts of the paragraph.

But external factors might be more influential. Black students and some other ethnic minorities might also suffer with the effects of poverty and material deprivation as many black families are single parent or on a low salary. Material deprivation will mean that these students don't have the best facilities at home to work in and the parents will not be able to afford extra books, revision materials etc. This might also link to cultural deprivation and a lack of money to expand their ideas and outlooks. Parents might also not value the British education system especially.

In Chinese and Indian families, children may become almost a personal project. These families are more likely to have extended families living nearby so this means that the children will be encouraged. Many families from this ethnic group own their own businesses and have a reputation for working hard. Their children will be socialised this way and it will help with their attitudes towards school. Lupton also found that in Asian families, parental respect was strong. This would help with behaviour and attitude in school. These children would be used to following a hierarchy and showing respect.

This is a clear description of an alternative view and a number of possible external factors are identified. There is no evidence to support any of these points, however, and some of them may be misleading. For example, plenty of evidence suggests that black and minority ethnic parents do place a high value on the education system in Britain and there is no attempt to distinguish between the circumstances of different ethnic groups (some of which may not be particularly materially deprived).

So there are both internal and external factors which are both important and hard to separate.

Some important points are made in this paragraph but most of it is quite generalised. Extended families don't necessarily result in greater encouragement and there is some confusion over whether the student is referring to one or more ethnic groups in the third sentence (they refer to this ethnic group in the singular having mentioned two ethnic groups at the beginning). However, some useful research is referenced towards the end of the paragraph.

This is a perfectly reasonable conclusion, but it is much too brief and the writer doesn't justify why it is hard to separate internal and external factors. Doing this would have been good analysis.

Overall, this is a competent answer. It has a basic structure and identifies a number of useful arguments both agreeing and disagreeing with the statement in the question. It is quite well-balanced between the competing viewpoints, it includes some sociological concepts and reference to several pieces of research. However, there are places where it is rather generalised, and it lacks detail and sophistication. For example, not much attempt is made to discuss the distinctive position of different ethnic groups or to look at the way that ethnicity intersects with class and gender. No detailed evidence is put forward to evaluate the competing points of view and the conclusion is very brief indeed. There is insufficient development for a 30-mark question to get into the top mark band.
**[Mark: 20/30]**

05  *Applying material from **Item C** and your own knowledge of research methods, evaluate the strengths and limitations of using questionnaires to investigate the role of parents in producing class differences in pupil attitudes to school.*  **[20 marks]**

Item C says that questionnaires can be a good way to reach parents. This is probably even more true in secondary schools where pupils are more likely to walk to school on their own or go by bus. In primary schools parents are more likely to be in the playground. So questionnaires are a good idea. But there are problems with this method.

Firstly parents' addresses will be confidential and the sociologist will not just be given this private information so they will have to find a way to get parents to agree, e.g. with a letter home. So it may be difficult to get many parents to agree. If the sample group is small this might affect the representativeness of the statistical data which is created.

Another problem with questionnaires is that parents may not answer honestly. This is a very sensitive issue and so parents may give socially desirable answers because they will not want to look like bad or irresponsible parents.

The answer starts with an immediate reference to the Item and thereby demonstrates application skills. There is a useful focus on the particular method in the particular context, although it is not applied particularly to studying educational achievement. A more substantial introduction would have been better, with some discussion of the nature of questionnaires and some background on the way that differential achievement can be studied.

These two short paragraphs both make good points about problems with using this method to study parents. The first paragraph starts off discussing practical concerns and goes on to consider a more theoretical issue, that is, the representativeness of the sample that will be generated. The second paragraph discusses a theoretical issue, concern with the validity of the data. There is scope to develop the analysis more here by explaining why it would be a sensitive issue and might, therefore, not have resulted in parents answering honestly. The points are quite brief and there is scope to develop further analysis.

Some evaluative points are made here which introduce some balance into the discussion. They are confined to practical issues, however, and the student could have discussed theoretical advantages such as being able to obtain a more representative sample than you tend to get using other research methods. While this paragraph focuses on using questionnaires to study parents of children in school, there is no discussion of the specific issue of studying differential achievement. For example, the student could have discussed questionnaires avoiding the problem of interviewer bias, which could result from the class of the interviewer (which could be evident from the way they dress and their accent).

But a good thing about questionnaires is that they can be cheap to create and to analyze. If lots of parents agree they can be given out quickly and do not take a lot of time like interviews and observations. People are more likely to agree to them.

Class might be an issue. Working-class parents might have jobs that involve less literacy or ethnically diverse parents might not speak English. They might have less understanding of the questions or feel embarrassed of low literacy levels. Middle-class parents are likely to be more supportive as they value education more, because they are more likely to have professional jobs and have been to university, but they may have less time.

There are some potentially important points here that are specific to the issue of class, but the student doesn't make it clear that they are discussing questionnaire research. There are some quite general assumptions made about class differences (for example the middle class have less time than the working class) and in any case the significance of these supposed differences is not spelt out for questionnaire research. It would have been better if the student had been more specific about how literacy problems might affect the response rate of parents from different classes. The final paragraph does not really act as a conclusion but makes a number of individual points of limited relevance because they are not directly applied to the question. This illustrates a general weakness in application to the question, application that is only partially successful, and a lack of depth in analysis and evaluation. Some technical terms are used in the answer, but there is room for more, and also for a more developed discussion of issues of validity, reliability and the merits of quantitative versus qualitative research.
**[Mark: 11/20]**

06 *Outline and explain two arguments against the view that participant observation produces valid data.* **[10 marks]**

Lots of people think that participant observation is more valid because sociologists are observing how groups really behave and in Weber's words, building up 'verstehen'.

This might not always be true though. If a sociologist does a participant observation study they can be overt or covert. If they are doing a covert study, then they are not revealing to the group what they are really doing. By joining the group, they may actually change some of the things that go on, the group dynamic and power relations. People might behave differently because someone new has joined the group. In James Patrick's study, some of the gang members did not get on with Patrick and so behaviour might have changed.

Another way it might not be valid is if it was an overt PO. This might mean that the group know there is someone in the group, but not the real intention of what's going on. This knowledge might also change the behaviour of the group and so they don't behave naturally and the results won't be valid.

The final paragraph essentially repeats the points in the second paragraph, but in the context of overt participant observation. The student could have made two distinct points if they had explained that overt and covert research could affect groups in different ways. In the case of covert research, the simple presence of the researcher could alter their behaviour, whereas in overt research the awareness of being studied is more likely to have an effect. However, it would have been much better to have made an entirely different point. For example, the student could have explained that participant observers have to be very selective when interpreting what they observe and writing up their findings. This means that the findings are likely to be strongly influenced by the preconceptions, mental categories and values of the researcher themselves, raising doubts about the validity of the data.

As it stands, the slightly repetitive nature of the discussion limits the overall mark.
[Mark: 5/10]

The first paragraph is a helpful way to start with a very brief introduction that demonstrates some relevant knowledge and an understanding of the view that participant observation may produce valid data.

The next paragraph makes a very good and relevant point about the potential the participant observer has to change the behaviour of the group because of their presence. As the student goes on to discuss, this doesn't apply only to covert observers but can apply to overt observers as well, indeed the latter are more likely to change the behaviour of the group because group members are aware that they are being observed. The first part of this paragraph, therefore, is not particularly relevant, which means that the relevant parts are quite undeveloped. However, a useful example is included and application to the question is good.

Total marks: 4 + 4 + 6 + 20 + 11 + 5 = 50/80 = 63% = C Grade

## Grade A answers

**01** *Outline **two** material factors that may affect gender differences in educational achievement.* [**4 marks**]

Firstly, parents may spend more money on providing a private education for boys than they do for girls. Traditionally, there are more private boys schools in the UK than private girls schools and the most prestigious and expensive schools are all-male ones such as Eton.

Secondly, parents may also spend more money on private tuition for sons than daughters. If they can't afford to send their children to private school, they may be able to afford extra tuition and it might be thought that boys need more help than girls who might be seen as more diligent. This might increase the educational achievement of boys relative to girls even if girls continue to do better overall.

Two factors are identified here and they are both clearly material factors because they involve money. They are distinctive enough to count as two separate factors and there is an explanation as to why they will result in gender differences in educational achievement. This could have been answered slightly more succinctly, but it achieves full marks.

**[Mark: 4/4]**

**02** *Outline **three ways** in which globalization has affected education in the UK.* [**6 marks**]

One way in which globalization has affected education is in the spread of new resources available for teaching. The internet has been revolutionary in education, spreading issues to a new global scale. Educational resources such as YouTube and other sites have changed the nature of teaching meaning that UK citizens can benefit from resources from elsewhere.

Secondly, globalization has arguably allowed greater access of people across borders, leading to academics being able to access universities in the UK more easily. For example, the Erasmus program has allowed the sharing of knowledge and information between universities and has also enabled more EU students from outside the UK to study in this country producing more cosmopolitan universities which may have benefited UK students by broadening their understanding of the world.

Thirdly, with globalization we have witnessed the spread and influence of business into education. For example, some degrees (particularly in sciences) can be funded by private companies in order to gain early access to the labour market and transnational educational corporations like Pearson are able to import business practices from other countries such as the USA.

The student clearly distinguishes three separate ways in which globalization has affected education and each of them is valid. Accessing international educational resources, making universities more cosmopolitan and importing business practices from abroad through transnational corporations are all good examples and they are explained well. They're not perhaps the most obvious examples of this or necessarily the most important, but there is no reason for the marker to deny full marks for this answer.

**[Mark: 6/6]**

03 *Applying material from **Item A**, analyse **two reasons** why some parents are unable to obtain places for their children in their first-choice school.* **[10 marks]**

Firstly, in existing grammar schools children may not pass the 11+ style exam to get in. Whilst grammar schools have been phased out, many survived the changes, for example in Lancaster. Places are determined by a selective examination. This divisive policy leads to excluding children from their, and their parents', first choice, and sending them off to what are regarded as 'second rate' schools. Furthermore, more privileged children are more likely to receive private coaching to pass an entrance exam so that even talented but poorer children will be unable to get into a grammar school.

Secondly, children may not be within a certain catchment area for the top-choice schools. Furthermore, those from working-class backgrounds may not be able to move to areas within the catchment area, leaving them at a disadvantage. House prices in the catchment areas for the most appealing schools tend to be quite high, both because the most successful schools tend to be in middle-class areas to start off with and also because people may be able to charge a premium when selling their houses because there is competition from parents to move into the area. Some free schools and faith schools may have a religious element to them. Consequently, proof of faith may be required.

The student applies material by making reference to grammar schools in the first part of the answer and demonstrates appropriate knowledge by commenting that some such schools have survived. There is a reference to the preferences of parents that also demonstrates good application skills and a clear explanation is given as to why some pupils will be denied entry even if the school is their preference. The second paragraph clearly explains why parents may not be able to move to the catchment area to get their children into the school of their choosing. Both parts of the answer contain analysis of how the mechanisms work to prevent parents from securing places in first-choice schools and go significantly beyond simply stating the reasons. There is almost enough development

This is another strong paragraph that is largely knowledge driven. It refers to three important studies. There is one mention of the Item, which helps demonstrate application skills and there is also some interesting analysis and evaluation. At the end of the paragraph, the student shows that processes such as labelling and stereotyping can be seen in a deterministic way and students can resist them in some circumstances. For these reasons, there is a good balance between different skills in this paragraph and the student avoids falling into the trap of simply describing without applying, analysing and evaluating.

These paragraphs broaden the case for factors internal to the education system being important and therefore help to move the argument forward. It is a slightly one-sided argument about the curriculum (for example the Civil Rights movement is certainly covered in some history courses today) but nevertheless reasonable points are made and are backed up with reference to research. The short section on subcultures is helpful but could be developed more and is also slightly one-sided. A little more detail might have made some of the arguments here more convincing and it would have been useful to have a direct reference to the Item. However, these are quite conceptually sophisticated paragraphs.

for full marks, but at the end of the answer the student goes into irrelevant material and introduces a third point (difficulties in getting into faith schools) which suggests slightly weak application skills. There is also room for a little evaluation of the importance of these reasons. **[Mark: 8/10]**

---

04   *Applying material from **Item B** and your own knowledge, evaluate the view that ethnic differences in educational achievement are mainly the result of factors inside school.*  **[30 marks]**

Ethnic groups are distinctive groups within society which have, to some extent, a shared culture and are believed by themselves or by others to share a common origin. Differences in educational achievement can be caused by factors internal to the education system (such as interaction between pupils and teachers and the organisation of schooling) or by external factors (such as material inequality and cultural differences). There are quite consistent patterns of inequality between ethnic groups though, as Item B suggests, these can change gradually over time. (For example the relative performance of Bangladeshi and Pakistani groups has improved over time.) This suggests that sociological factors may be at work and the data in Item B demonstrates that you should not generalise about all minority ethnic groups underperforming in education.

This is a good start which defines the key terms in the question and analyses the factors that might lead to ethnic differences in educational achievement. It also analyses some key features of patterns of educational achievement by ethnicity and makes a sophisticated point about the way the evidence points to sociological influences on achievement. Application skills are demonstrated through the direct reference to the Item and it is good that the student begins to analyze issues in the first paragraph.

However, several internal factors may affect several ethnic minority groups. Firstly, teachers may have negative expectations of those from ethnic minorities in education, due to false and negative stereotypes. This may lead to a lack of support and a self-fulfilling prophecy in attainment. Studies from Gillborn and Youdell support this, claiming a culture of institutional racism exists within school with racialised expectations which helped explain high rates of exclusion and placement in low sets for Black Caribbean pupils. Gillborn and Youdell acknowledge (as Item B notes) that racism is not always intentional, but this does not alter the significant effects it can have. As stated by the Item, black children are likely to be discriminated against. For example, they are more likely to be placed in lower sets. Wright also studied attention given to students in primary schools. Those from the African-Caribbean community were far more likely to receive negative attention from teachers, ☞

as they expected them to behave badly. Gender stereotypes also played a role in interaction with ethnic/racial stereotypes, with boys often seen as aggressive and were discriminated against by teachers. However, it should be remembered that pupils do not always live up to stereotypes and can reject them, as shown in research by both Margaret Fuller and Mac an Ghaill. Pupils have agency and don't always respond passively.

Nevertheless, the curriculum in schools is often highly ethno-centric, thus denying those from ethnic minority their identity. As Stephen Ball argues, this is particularly persistent in history teaching. Curriculum is dominated by European and US history from a high-political perspective. Research shows that those from the black community were often denied agency in this version of history. Where they were present in history classes was in slavery. Black people are usually represented as passive entities in history, particularly under slavery. This denies the positive aspects of history, for example the civil rights movement.

Furthermore, the formation of subcultures within education can affect educational achievement. This is often a response to institutional racism. For example, Louise Archer demonstrated how Muslim boys develop somewhat distinct (it drew partly on Black 'gangsta' culture) and somewhat anti-school subcultures as a response to what they viewed as Islamophobia.

Whilst in-school factors are important, they alone do not account for the ethnic inequality in education. Societal factors are extremely pertinent when explaining ethnicity and attainment in education. This is certainly the case with material factors. For example, research suggests that white working class boys are the lowest achievers at school. This is largely due to under-funding in de-industrialised areas with high rates of poverty. Those from households with low income often have a poor environment at home for studying. Furthermore, they may rely on food-banks and are not receiving sufficient nutrition to do well at school. Lack of sustenance can affect concentration levels and attainment in school. Low income can also affect minority ethnic groups. Research by Strand suggests that those from the Afro-Caribbean community often were from low-income households. This also meant less access to equipment such as computers at home. Material factors may also help to explain the success of pupils of Indian origin compared with those of Pakistani and Bangladeshi communities as their parents are less likely to be in professional and managerial employment.

Other factors such as cultural aspiration may also lead to differences in educational attainment. Those from the Chinese community perform the highest in the British education system. This may be due to strong emphasis from households to achieve through education. Research by Archer and Francis suggested that this could help to account for the success of this group.

Overall, in-school factors are fundamentally important in determining the correlation between ethnicity and educational attainment. This affects teaching in the classroom, the likelihood of punishment for bad behaviour, and the setting system. However, arguably external societal factors are equally important when explaining ethnicity and attainment in education. Funding for ☞

These paragraphs are crucial to developing an evaluative essay because they put the other side of the argument that factors external to schools might cause ethnic differences in achievement. The first paragraph starts off a little vaguely but then includes some more specific evidence to support the claims being made. The discussion of cultural factors is quite brief but again is supported by specific research that helps to broaden the discussion. This material is clearly relevant and some of the higher-level skills of analysis and evaluation are being demonstrated. However, early on more specific knowledge could have been included and application could have been stronger with one or more references to the Item.

Part of this paragraph drifts away from the question and starts to focus on social class rather than ethnicity as such. However, when the student begins to talk about the interaction of different social divisions (intersectionality), the analysis and application become much better. The evaluation towards the end is excellent. The student argues for a distinct position (that you can't disentangle the separate effects of internal and external factors) and takes quite a subtle and sophisticated stance. This is backed up very well with an example from named research.

This paragraph lacks an introduction to the answer and it would be a better structured answer with an introduction. However, the student quickly gets into their stride identifying strengths of the method. Initially, they make a point about using questionnaires with parents and they therefore apply their discussion well to the question although they don't make specific reference to using questionnaires to study class. The next part of the paragraph applies the material well in the educational context. A particularly strong point suggests that the possibility of a large sample means that questionnaires are useful for studying smaller social classes and – in the section discussing free schools – class, education and questionnaires are integrated together successfully. After some general points, the student again focuses on class issues and makes an excellent point about the limitations of official statistics, which tend to be based on eligibility for free school meals. There is a reasonable balance between discussing practical, ethical and theoretical issues although these could have been distinguished more clearly.

schools in certain areas may explain the lack of attainment – with education cuts being made, particularly for schools run by councils. External factors in the home also have a large impact. Those from working-class backgrounds have less access to materials important for homework, and may be materially deprived of basic amenities, such as affordable transport to schools and a decent nutritional diet. Furthermore, ethnicity interacts with other social divisions in processes of intersectionality including social class and gender. Ultimately, it is difficult to disentangle the impact of external and internal factors and determine which is more important because they too can interact and sometimes reinforce one another. For example, Archer and Francis found that parental support for pupils of Chinese ethnic origin influenced teachers so they had a generally positive attitude to these pupils which may have further reinforced the positive attitude of parents.

Overall this is a sound and conceptually detailed answer where material has generally been chosen well and applied sensitively to the question. Analysis and evaluation is explicit and relevant and the student certainly draws appropriate conclusions based upon the arguments they have put forward. Therefore, this answer gets into the top mark band (25–30) but there are some weaknesses in the application skills and at times the analysis and knowledge could have been a little sharper.
**[Mark: 26/30]**

**05** *Applying material from **Item C** and your own knowledge of research methods, evaluate the strengths and limitations of using questionnaires to investigate the role of parents in producing class differences in pupil attitudes to school.* **[20 marks]**

As the Item suggests, one strength of using questionnaires is that they will be relatively cost-effective and simple to use. Gaining access would be much easier than interviewing parents if schools allow letters with questionnaires to be taken home with pupils. This will make it easier to have a wider sample base, and therefore establish a broader analysis across different geographical areas which have different characteristics. This will allow for comparison of results, for example between different types of schools such as grammars, Free schools and academies (which may have different local educational markets). Furthermore, they also provide a large amount of quantitative data. This is useful for establishing trends and making generalization, perhaps including those relating to relatively small social classes in the class structure. This method would allow for longitudinal studies to see results across time and space. For example, you could look at how the introduction of a new free school affected the impact of parents' social class on achievement. This is useful for understanding patterns within a changing society. If questionnaires allow for elaboration on a point, this may also grant useful qualitative data, useful for understanding cultural interpretations. A particular benefit is ☞

that questionnaires allow preliminary questions on class which make it possible to classify parents in terms of their social class and not in terms of whether they are entitled to free school meals (a measure of low income rather than class as such) which is used in official statistics. Furthermore, most of the factors in play, whether material or cultural, are often of a personal nature and you may get more valid answer using anonymous questionnaires without an interviewer present.

However, there are severe limitations with this method. Firstly, the stratification of class is methodologically hard to operationalise in questionnaires. Class represents a complex set of material factors, primarily on income and wealth, but also in terms of area of habitation. Class is also a social construction, in that it is highly interwoven with people's identity. Consequently, parents from the same school might have similar material backgrounds, but may culturally situate themselves as 'working class' or 'middle class'. A questionnaire does not allow for a deeper understanding of class as a cultural phenomenon and how this might affect attitudes to education. Studies such as interviews or participant observation may be more useful for understanding the nuances of class as an identity and how this affects the nature and amount of encouragement or support given to children by parents. Secondly, the agenda of parents may shape results: for example, parents of children who go to private schools may deny their cultural capital as an important factor relating to attainment if they don't want to feel their children have an unfair advantage. This can affect the validity of the findings. Understanding the phenomenon of cultural capital would require more in-depth research, for example conducting interviews or observation of daily life within households. Thirdly, there may be ethical issues about anonymity if the researchers want to match the questionnaire results with details of the attainment of pupils. Fourthly, the response rate for questionnaires, particularly those sent home with pupils (which may not even reach parents) raising problems with reliability. For these reasons, questionnaires are useful for practical purposes in this context, and it may be impossible to gain access to a large sample of parents using any other method, but the findings may lack depth on the subjective experience of class and how this directly and indirectly affects attainment.

This paragraph balances the first paragraph by going on to examine the second part of the question – the limitations of using questionnaires to study parents, class and differential achievement. There is some quite sophisticated discussion of the nature of social class, which raises questions about relying exclusively on quantitative data to study parental attitudes. The student is quite specific about the context in which the use of questionnaires is being discussed and therefore demonstrates very good analytical and application skills. The paragraph is also very evaluative. The point about ethical issues is also very well applied to the specific study area while the point about response rate picks up on issues related to using questionnaires with parents. Although this answer lacks an introduction, there is a brief but very effective conclusion that rounds the answer off well.

Overall, this is a very strong answer showing a good knowledge and understanding; it is quite conceptually sophisticated, there is ample analysis, balanced evaluation and a reasoned conclusion. There are times when the answer is extremely well applied to the question because it doesn't just analyse the strengths and limitations of questionnaires but considers the context, the group and the topic to be studied. It could have been improved with the addition of a brief introduction and more direct references to the Item, but it still comes close to achieving full marks.

**[Mark: 18/20]**

**06** *Outline and explain two arguments against the view that participant observation produces valid data.* **[10 marks]**

Firstly, participant observation, by definition, requires the intervention of the researcher into the lives of those they are studying. This undoubtedly will lead to alterations in the behaviour of participants. For example, if someone who is considered as having high status or authority, then participants may shift their behaviour to act more reasonably as to not harm their own reputation. Consequently, the results will not be as valid as if the observation is based on non-participation: the data will have been distorted by the research process.

This is because interactions between people will have been altered compared to when they are in their 'normal' state. Consequently, they may be invalid in helping sociologists making judgements about society as a whole.

Secondly, it is difficult for researchers in participant observation to accurately record what they are experiencing. If the research is covert, it would be difficult for the researcher to record with a camera, or to write down in detail what is happening, so as not to blow their cover. If it was blown the research might have to be cut short. If data is being recorded from memory, this may be a flawed description and analysis of events and the interactions involved. Overall, it would be far more difficult to defend the data as giving a true representation of what occurred if recalled from memory, rather than being recorded or noted at the time.

The student gives two clear and distinct arguments, suggesting that participant observation may produce invalid data. Although neither is developed in tremendous detail, they demonstrate a very good understanding of what is meant by validity and both points are logically argued and very well applied to the question. The analysis can't really be faulted here, so this answer would gain full marks.

Overall this is an excellent answer that would comfortably achieve an A grade. Although there are some areas for improvement at the margin, the student has demonstrated an excellent command of the subject as well as the ability to apply material to questions and to analyze and evaluate in their answers.
**[Mark: 10/10]**

**Total mark: 4 + 6 + 8 + 9 + 14 = 72/80 = 90% = Grade A**

## Education and Research Methods

| | |
|---|---|
| **Academies** | Schools that are independent of local authority control, set up by the Labour government of 1997 to 2010 in inner-cities, and schools that opted out of local authority control under the coalition government from 2010 |
| **Achieved status** | A position in society that affects the way others view you that is earned, at least partly, through your own efforts, e.g. a job |
| **Alienation** | A sense of being distanced from something so that it feels alien, e.g. feeling a lack of connection and fulfilment in work |
| **Anti-school subcultures** | **Subcultures** opposed to the dominant **values** of a school |
| **Ascribed status** | A position in society that affects the way others view you which you get at birth, e.g. being male or female |
| **Attainment gap** | Any percentage difference between two groups in terms of them achieving a particular educational standard, for example, the gap between those who are and those who are not receiving free school meals in terms of gaining five or more good GCSEs |
| **Attitudes survey** | A **survey** collecting information about subjective opinions |
| **Authenticity** | How genuine **documents** are |
| **Availability** | Whether documents have survived and are accessible to researchers |
| **Bands/banding** | Placing pupils into broad groups according to their general academic ability |
| **Bourgeoisie** | The **ruling class** in capitalist societies who own property such as **capital**, businesses and shares |
| **Breadwinner** | The person in a household who is paid the most for work |
| **Capital** | Assets that can be used to produce more resources |
| **Capitalist society/ capitalism** | A society in which people are employed for wages, and in which businesses are set up with the aim of making a profit |
| **Catchment area** | The geographical area from which pupils eligible to attend the school are drawn |
| **Causal relationship** | When one thing causes another |
| **Case study** | An individual example of something that is studied in depth |
| **Census** | A **social survey** carried out by the government every 10 years in the UK, collecting standardized data about the whole population |
| **City Technology Colleges** | New schools set up in inner-cities with an emphasis on scientific and technical subjects along with maths. Independent of **LEAs** and partly funded by businesses |
| **Class/social class** | Groups within society distinguished by their economic position and that are therefore unequal, e.g. the **middle class** in better paid, non-manual jobs and the **working class** in less well-paid, physical jobs |
| **Class subculture** | The distinctive lifestyle associated with a particular class |
| **Collaborative interviewing** | Interviewing in which the interviewees become full partners in the research |
| **Collectivist** | Putting the interests of the social group before the interests of the individual |
| **Compensatory education** | Additional education provided to try to address underperformance by particular social groups in the education system |

| | |
|---|---|
| **Complementarity** | Where different methods are combined to dovetail different aspects of an investigation |
| **Comprehensive school** | A type of school attended by all children regardless of ability or aptitude |
| **Confidentiality** | Keeping data secret |
| **Conflict theory** | Theory of society that sees one or more groups in competition for scarce or valued goods, examples include marxism and **feminism** |
| **Content analysis** | Research in which the written, spoken or visual content of the mass media is analysed |
| **Control group** | In an **experiment**, a group in which **variables** are not changed so that the effects of changing one variable in another group can be determined |
| **Correlation** | A statistical tendency for two things to be found together |
| **Correspondence principle** | In the **Marxist** theory of Bowles and Gintis, the idea that the structure, organization and values of educational institutions reflect, or correspond to, the structure, organization and values of the workplace in capitalist businesses |
| **Counterculture** | The beliefs and lifestyle of a group who are opposed to the dominant culture |
| **Counter-school culture** | The beliefs of a group who are opposed to the values of those in authority at a school |
| **Covert participant observation** | **Participant observation** where researchers do not reveal to the people being observed that they are conducting research |
| **Cream-skimming** | Schools or other educational institutions selecting the most able pupils/students to attend their institution |
| **Crisis in masculinity** | The idea that clear roles for men in society no longer exist as a result of the decline in male-dominated manual work or changes in society's **culture** |
| **Cultural capital** | Non-material assets such as your social class or how you spend your leisure time or dress, which are valued by society and can be helpful in achieving educational success |
| **Cultural deprivation** | Lacking or being deficient in the attitudes, values, knowledge, linguistic ability or lifestyles necessary to succeed in the education system |
| **Cultural factors** | Factors concerned with lifestyle, attitudes and values that might affect achievement in education, as opposed to **material factors** |
| **Culture** | The **norms**, values, attitudes and lifestyle of a social group |
| **Curriculum** | The formal content of what is taught in schools and other educational institutions |
| **Deferred gratification** | Putting off pleasure now in order to achieve greater pleasure in the future, e.g. saving for a deposit on a house |
| **Deterministic** | A theory that sees behaviour as entirely determined by external circumstances, leaving the individual with little or no choice about how they behave |
| **Deviants** | People who do not abide by the norms of society |
| **Differential educational achievement** | Systematic differences in the performance of social groups in the education system, e.g. between **social classes** |
| **Disconnected choosers** | Parents who lack the skills and resources to exercise choice effectively in the education system |
| **Division of labour** | The way in which jobs are divided up between two or more people, e.g. who does particular tasks in a household |

| | |
|---|---|
| **Documents** | Any physical artefacts containing information that could be used by sociologists as a source of data |
| **Dominant culture** | The culture that is most powerful and has the highest status in a society |
| **Economic base** | In Marxist theory, the foundation of society consisting of the economic system |
| **Economic capital** | Material assets such as housing and income that can be helpful in achieving educational success |
| **Education Action Zones** | Areas of deprived inner-cities where additional compensatory education schemes were started in the 1970s |
| **Educational triage** | The rationing of education so that only those who are likely to attain targets through receiving extra help are provided with additional assistance |
| **Efficiency** | Achieving the best possible outcomes using the least possible resources |
| **Egoism** | According to Durkheim, a situation when people are not well integrated into social groups and therefore are mainly concerned with themselves rather than others |
| **Elaborated codes** | A type of speech where the meanings are filled in and made explicit. Sentences tend to be longer and more complex than in **restricted codes** |
| **Equality of opportunity equal opportunities** | When every individual has an equal chance of success based upon their own ability and effort. Will tend to lead to inequality of outcome, i.e. some people will be more successful than others because they are more able or they work harder |
| **Ethical factors / issues** | Factors concerned with morality |
| **Ethnic group** | A group within a population regarded by themselves or by others as culturally distinctive – they usually see themselves as having a common origin |
| **Ethnographic study** | The study of the lifestyle of a group of people |
| **Experiment** | An artificial situation set up by a researcher in order to test a **hypothesis** |
| **Explanatory survey** | A **survey** testing theories or hypotheses |
| **External rewards** | Things that are given to someone in recognition of their efforts, e.g. wages or exam certificates – this is in contrast to internal rewards such as personal satisfaction or happiness |
| **Facilitation** | Where one method is used to assist or develop use of another method |
| **Factual survey** | A **survey** collecting descriptive information |
| **Falsify/falsification** | Proving something wrong |
| **Fatalism** | A belief that your chances in life are shaped by luck or fate rather than believing you can determine them by you own efforts |
| **Femininity** | The social roles and behaviour expected of women in a particular culture |
| **Feminism/feminist** | Theory of society that claims that women are disadvantaged and exploited by men, while men are dominant and run society in their own interests |
| **Field experiments** | An experiment conducted in a natural social setting rather than in a laboratory |
| **Fixed-choice questions** | Questions where the respondent has to choose from a range of predetermined responses |
| **Focus group** | A group interview used to collect data on opinions and attitudes |

| Formal content analysis | Analysis of mass media content in which numerical data is produced about the frequency of different types of content appearing in a source |
|---|---|
| Formal curriculum | The official content (subject and courses) of educational institutions |
| Fragmented | Divided into small pieces so that no coherent whole exists |
| Fragmented centralization | The process whereby the government gives more independence or autonomy to individual schools but takes increasing central control of some aspects of education policy, for example, the curriculum |
| Free market | A system in which businesses can compete with one another without state interference |
| Free schools | Schools set up by charities, teachers, businesses or parents but funded by the **state**. They were introduced after 2010 |
| Functionalism | A sociological view that social institutions serve some positive purpose |
| Functionally important jobs | Occupations that are believed to play a particularly crucial role in the effective functioning of society |
| Future-time orientation | Thinking ahead rather than living in the moment |
| Functions | Useful jobs performed by an institution for society |
| Gender gap | The difference in the achievement of boys and girls in the education system |
| Gender roles | The socially expected behaviour of men and women in a particular society |
| Gender socialization | The way in which men and women are taught to behave differently in a particular society |
| Generalizability | Statements about a wider population on the basis of a particular **sample** |
| Globalization | The process by which national borders and distance become less important in social processes as the world becomes a more integrated place |
| Grammar schools | Secondary schools in which admission is granted on the basis of ability – originally measured through an IQ test, the 11+ |
| Grant-maintained schools | Schools funded directly by government, independent of LEAs |
| Group interview | An **interview** where several interviewees are questioned together |
| Habitus | The dispositions, tastes and lifestyles associated with a particular social class |
| Hawthorne effect | When people being observed in observational research or an experiment change their behaviour because they are aware that they are being monitored |
| Hegemony/ hegemonic | Political or cultural dominance |
| Hidden curriculum | The hidden, informal messages and lessons outside the formal curriculum that come from the way schooling is organized |
| Hierarchy | Where individuals are ranked above and below one another, and orders and instructions flow from the top of the hierarchy towards the bottom |
| Hypothesis | A statement to be tested through research |
| Ideal pupil | The image held by teachers of the sort of pupil they would choose to have in their classes if they were allowed to select those whom they taught |

| | |
|---|---|
| **Ideology** | A distorted set of beliefs that favour the interests of a particular social group |
| **Immediate gratification** | Enjoying yourself now, e.g. spending your wage packet as soon as you get it |
| **Income** | Money received by an individual or social group |
| **Individual achievement** | When each person is primarily concerned for their own success rather than the success of a social group as a whole |
| **Individualism** | An emphasis upon the desires or interests of individual people rather than those of wider social groups |
| **Industrialization** | The process whereby manufacturing takes over from agriculture as the most important component in a society's economy |
| **Industrial society** | A society that has undergone the process of industrialization |
| **Inequality of opportunity** | When some individuals or groups have more chance of success than others because of unfair advantages |
| **Informed consent** | Agreeing to take part in research while being fully aware of the purpose of the research and its implications |
| **Infrastructure** | In Marxist theory, the foundation of society consisting of the economic system (same as **economic base**) |
| **Institutional racism** | 'The collective failure of an organization to provide an appropriate and professional service to people because of their colour, culture, or ethnic origin' (MacPherson, 1999) |
| **Interactionism** | An interpretivist sociological perspective that emphasizes **meanings**, **motives** and **self-concepts** |
| **Interpretative understanding/ interpretivist** | Being able to understand what a document means |
| **Interview** | A research method in which one or more people ask an individual or group a series of questions |
| **Interviewer bias** | When the results of interviews are distorted by the presence or behaviour of the interviewer |
| **IQ test** | An intelligence test designed to test a person's abstract reasoning ability rather than their knowledge of subjects |
| **Key informant** | A respondent or interviewee who is particularly helpful to a researcher |
| **Label/labelling** | The qualities or the identity conferred on a person or social group through the expressed opinions of others |
| **Labour market** | The overall structure of the market in which employers and workers buy and sell labour |
| **Laws** | Statements about universal relationships of cause and effect |
| **League tables** | Tables ranking schools in terms of their performance in exams or by other criteria |
| **LEAs** | Local Education Authorities responsible for running most aspects of the education system in a particular area |
| **Left wing** | Political views that favour greater equality through the redistribution of wealth and income from rich to poor, and which support state intervention in the economy |
| **Legitimate** | Used as a verb – to make something seem fair and reasonable. Used as a noun – something that is accepted as fair and reasonable |

| Liberal feminism | A version of feminism that is relatively moderate and believes that the position of women in society can be improved through reform rather than radical or revolutionary change |
|---|---|
| Life course | The development and change in people's lives over periods of time. Unlike the life-cycle, the life course does not have fixed and predictable stages |
| Life documents | Private documents created by individuals and used to record their thoughts and feelings |
| Life history | An in-depth study of an individual's life |
| Literal understanding | Being able to read, decipher or translate the content of a document |
| Longitudinal study | A study that takes place over an extended period of time, often with periodic gathering of data |
| Manual labour/ manual jobs | Work that primarily involves physical effort rather than thought |
| Marketization | Introducing competition into education, along with formula funding, so that educational institutions start to act like businesses |
| Market liberal | Another term for **neoliberals** who believe the **free market** is a good thing |
| Marxist | Person following the theory of Karl Marx that argues that societies are dominated by a ruling class that owns the **means of production** |
| Masculinity | The behaviour and social roles expected of men in a particular culture |
| Material factors | Factors to do with money and other material resources (e.g. housing) that might affect performance in education, as opposed to cultural factors |
| Material resources | Physical and financial possessions that are useful in achieving objectives such as success in education |
| Meanings | The interpretations made by people of acts, words or other symbols, in the context of evaluating documents |
| Means of production | Those things required to produce goods such as land, machinery, capital, technical knowledge and workers |
| Merit | Worth judged in terms of ability and effort |
| Meritocracy/ meritocratic society | A society in which people's positions, e.g. their jobs, are determined on merit, i.e. according to their abilities and how hard they have worked |
| Methodology | The methods used to collect data and the philosophy underlying the production of sociological data |
| Middle class | People who have white-collar jobs that require some qualifications and are generally better paid than the **working class** |
| Migration | The movements of people between different geographical areas |
| Mixed ability | A class where all pupils are taught together regardless of their level of ability |
| Mode of production | The dominant system of producing things in a society, e.g. capitalism |
| Moral panic | A sudden and illogical outburst of public concern about some perceived decline in the moral standards of society, the implication being that the concern is exaggerated or does not match reality |

| Motives | The subjective reasons for behaving in particular ways |
|---|---|
| **Multicultural curriculum** | A curriculum that reflects the lifestyles (e.g. religions), history and interests of pupils/students from different ethnic groups |
| **Multi-stage sampling** | Sampling in which a sample of a sample is taken, e.g. a sample of voters in a sample of constituencies |
| **National Curriculum** | Subjects and subject content laid down by central government, which it is compulsory for schools to teach. First introduced in 1988 |
| **Neoliberal** | Politicians, thinkers and writers who support the free market rather than state intervention and who believe that traditional moral values should be preserved |
| **Neo-Marxism** | New versions of Marxism that are strongly influenced by the works of Karl Marx but disagree with some aspects of them and have been updated to fit contemporary society |
| **New Labour** | The Labour Party under the leadership of Tony Blair and Gordon Brown, which distanced itself from previous **social democratic** policies and instead adopted the **Third Way** |
| **New Right** | Those who believe in the free market |
| **Non-directive interviewing** | Interviewing in which the interviewer does not reveal their own opinions or suggest answers to the respondents |
| **Non-manual labour** | Work that does not primarily require physical effort, e.g. office work |
| **Non-representative sampling** | A sampling technique in which people who are not typical of a wider population are chosen |
| **Norms** | Specific, informal rules of behaviour in a particular society |
| **Objectivity** | Making true statements about the world, not influenced by personal opinion or preferences |
| **Observation** | A research method in which one or more researchers watch individuals or social groups and record their data |
| **Occupational groups** | Clusters of similar jobs, e.g. professional or **service sector** jobs. Occupational groups are sometimes used as a way of distinguishing **social classes** |
| **Official statistics** | Numerical data produced by government agencies |
| **Open-ended questions** | Questions where the respondents may give whatever response they think fit and do not have to choose from predetermined options |
| **Operationalizing** | Defining a concept in a form that can be measured, usually by identifying a series of indicators |
| **Opportunity sampling** | Sampling in which people are chosen because they happen to be easily accessible and willing to participate in the research |
| **Oversubscribed school** | A school that more pupils wish to attend than there are places available |
| **Overt participant observation** | Participant observation where the researcher is open about the fact that they are conducting research |
| **Panel study** | A longitudinal study, used to collect data from a sample of people over a number of years |

| Participant observation | Research conducted by observing a group while taking part in its activities |
|---|---|
| Particularistic standards | When people are judged as particular individuals, e.g. parents judging children |
| Partly structured interviews | An interview in which there are a small number of preset questions or list of topics that need to be covered |
| Patriarchy/ patriarchal | Literally 'rule by the father', usually used by **feminists** to refer to a system in which men have more power than women and shape how societies run |
| Peer group | A group of people with a similar **status**, and often age, to whom you compare yourself and who may influence your behaviour |
| Pilot study | A preliminary small-scale trial study carried out before the main research in order to test the feasibility of the main study and to refine the research methods being used |
| Population | The total group the sociologist is interested in when conducting research |
| Positivism | A philosophy of social research based upon scientific ideas of **objectivity** |
| Practical factor/ issue | A factor in research to do with time, money or access as opposed to **ethical** or **theoretical issues** |
| Pre-industrial society | Societies that existed before industrialization in which most production was based upon agriculture |
| Private documents | Documents produced by individuals, not normally available to members of the public |
| Privatization | The process by which state-owned or state-run businesses/services are taken over by private sector companies |
| Privileged/skilled choosers | Parents who have the resources and skills necessary to make effective choices in the education system |
| Present-time orientation | Living life in the moment rather than worrying about the future |
| Primary data source | Data collected by sociologists themselves |
| Primary socialization | The first stage of the process in which children learn the culture of their society, it takes place in the family |
| Private enterprise | **Businesses** owned by individuals or shareholders and run in order to make a profit |
| Private schools | Schools run by non-state organizations where pupils have to pay to attend |
| Progressive taxation | A taxation policy designed to reduce inequality in society by taking more tax from those on high incomes than from those on low incomes |
| Public documents | Documents that are readily available to members of the public |
| Public schools | High status and expensive private schools in Britain |
| Pupil premium | Extra money given to schools for disadvantaged pupils entitled to free school meals and introduced by the government of 2010–15 |
| Qualitative data | Data that takes a non-numerical form, e.g. words and images |
| Quantitative data | Data that takes a numerical form |
| Questionnaire | A written list of questions |

| | |
|---|---|
| **Quota sampling** | A system in which quotas are established, which determine how many people with particular characteristics are studied. Once a quota is filled, no more people in that category are included |
| **Racism** | Discriminatory beliefs or actions based upon a person's supposed 'race' or ethnic group |
| **Random sampling** | A system in which every sampling unit has an equal chance of being chosen, e.g. drawn out of a hat |
| **Relative autonomy** | In Marxist theory, a degree of independence – particularly when parts of the **superstructure** have some independence from the economic base and the ruling class |
| **Reliability** | Data is reliable if another researcher using identical methods would produce the same results |
| **Representativeness** | How typical the data is of a wider population |
| **Replication** | Producing a copy of something – particularly repeating research to check results |
| **Response rate** | The proportion of selected subjects who take go on to part in research, e.g. by returning a questionnaire |
| **Restricted codes** | A type of shorthand speech where meanings are not made fully explicit – it uses short, simple and often unfinished sentences |
| **Right wing** | Political views that tend to favour free markets over state intervention, support competition, and therefore believe that inequality is an inevitable part of society |
| **Role allocation** | Determining which individuals carry out which roles, e.g. deciding who does what jobs |
| **Ruling class** | In Marxist theory, the group who are dominant in society by virtue of their wealth and power |
| **Sample** | A group selected from within a wider population with whom research is carried out |
| **Sampling frame** | A list of individual **sampling units** from which a sample is drawn |
| **Sampling unit** | The individual person or thing that is the subject of research and is selected to be part of a sample from a population |
| **Secondary data/ source** | Existing data used by sociologists rather than data derived from research |
| **Secondary modern schools** | Schools attended by students who failed to get into selective grammar schools. Focus on vocational, rather than academic, education |
| **Selective schools** | Schools that can choose some or all of their pupils on the basis of ability, or some other criteria |
| **Self-concept** | The way individuals see or define themselves |
| **Self-fulfilling prophecy** | Something that occurs because somebody has predicted that it will happen |
| **Semi-structured interviews** | Type of interview that combines open and fixed-choice questions and/or where the structure gives the interviewer flexibility in their choice and wording of questions |
| **Service sector** | Parts of the economy involved in providing services to people rather than manufacturing goods |
| **Set/setting** | Placing pupils in groups according to their ability in a particular subject |
| **Sexism** | Discriminatory beliefs or actions based upon a person's sex |
| **Sex stereotyping** | Treating males and females according to widely held **stereotypes** of typical behaviour |

| | |
|---|---|
| **Shop-floor culture** | The attitudes and behaviour of workers in factories and similar places of work, particularly behaviour by men |
| **Sincerity** | Whether the author of a document intends to provide a true account or to mislead their readers |
| **Sites of ideological struggle** | Places where there is conflict between competing beliefs; e.g. between the belief that an equally good education should be provided for all students and the one that most money should go to the best students |
| **Snowballing** | A sampling technique in which a member of a sample puts the researcher in touch with other potential members to include in the sample |
| **Social capital** | The possession of valuable social contacts that can assist in achieving success in education |
| **Social construction** | A behaviour or practice that is produced by society even though it may seem natural or biological |
| **Social democrat** | A political viewpoint associated with the traditional Labour Party that supports creating greater equality by reforming **capitalist** society. Associated with the introduction of comprehensive schools |
| **Social facts** | Facts about social phenomena |
| **Social mobility** | The movement of people between social groups, especially social classes |
| **Social solidarity** | A sense of belonging, commitment and loyalty to a social group |
| **Socialization** | The process through which people learn the culture of their society |
| **Soundness** | Whether a document is complete and is reliable |
| **State** | The practices and institutions directly or indirectly controlled by the government and its bureaucracy in a country |
| **Status** | The amount of esteem in which people are held by others in society |
| **Stereotype** | A simplified and usually highly misleading image of a social group |
| **Stratified random sampling** | A system of sampling in which the population is divided into groups according to important **variables** such as **class**, gender and **ethnicity,** and the sample is then chosen in the same proportions as they exist in the population |
| **Streams/streaming** | Placing pupils in groups according to their general academic ability |
| **Structured interview** | An interview in which questions are predetermined |
| **Subculture** | A group within a wider culture that has significantly different **norms**, attitudes, values and lifestyle to other groups in society, while sharing some aspects of the wider culture |
| **Subject class** | In Marxist theory, the group in society who are dominated by the ruling class whom they have to work for because they lack the property to produce goods for themselves. The subject class is exploited by the ruling class |
| **Superstructure** | In Marxist theory, the non-economic parts of society such as the family, which are shaped by the economy and controlled by the ruling class |
| **Sure Start** | Schemes to provide additional pre-school education and extra educational resources, including help for parents, in deprived, inner-city areas |
| **Surplus value** | Profits made by the ruling class |
| **Survey/ social survey** | Research collecting standardized information about a large group of people |

| | |
|---|---|
| **Symbolic capital** | Possession of high social status, e.g. that which comes from having an image of respectability |
| **Technical schools** | Schools for those believed to have technical talents set up as part of the **tripartite system** |
| **Textual analysis** | The detailed analysis of small pieces of text in the mass media |
| **Thematic analysis** | Analysis of the mass media in which the underlying message of the coverage of a particular topic is interpreted |
| **Theoretical factors/ issues** | Factors concerned with the quality of information produced in research |
| **Third Way** | The philosophy of the New Labour Party, which claims to steer a middle way between left-wing and right-wing politics |
| **Triangulation** | The use of several different research methods in one study |
| **Tripartite system** | The system of secondary **state** education set up in Britain in 1944 in which children went to one of three types of school – grammar, secondary modern or technical |
| **Typology** | A classification of different types of a phenomenon |
| **Underachievement** | Doing less well than your potential suggests you should do in the education system |
| **Universalistic standards** | When people are judged according to an abstract set of standards, e.g. when exams are being marked |
| **Unstructured interview** | An interview in which there are no or very few predetermined questions |
| **Upper class** | The highest social class in society, consisting of those who own wealth or property |
| **Upward social mobility** | Moving from one social class to a higher class |
| **Values** | General beliefs about what is right or wrong in a particular society |
| **Validity** | How true data is, i.e. how close the fit is between the data and reality |
| **Variable** | A cause or an effect, something that can produce a change or can be changed |
| **Vocational** | Related to jobs, i.e. education designed to provide the skills necessary for work |
| **Within-class groupings** | Teaching where pupils are divided into different ability groups in the same classroom |
| **Working class** | People who do manual jobs that require relatively few qualifications and who are usually less well-paid than those with middle-class jobs |
| **Youth culture** | A subculture associated with a group of young people, particularly those associated with particular ways of dressing or musical tastes |

# Index

# Notes

# Notes

# Notes